Achievement Testing

in the

Early Grades:

The Games Grown-Ups Play

Constance Kamii, Editor

A 1989–1990 Comprehensive Membership benefit

**National Association for
the Education of Young Children
Washington, D.C.**

National Association for the Education of Young Children
1834 Connecticut Ave., N.W.
Washington, DC 20009-5786

The National Association for the Education of Young Children attempts through its publications program to provide a forum for discussion of major issues and ideas in our field. We hope to provoke thought and promote professional growth. The views expressed or implied are not necessarily those of the Association.

Library of Congress Catalog Card Number: 89-064092
ISBN: 0-935989-32-3
NAEYC #340

Cover design: Polly Greenberg
Interior design and production: Jack Zibulsky

Printed in the United States of America

Contents

About the Authors

Constance Kamii is Professor of Early Childhood Education at the University of Alabama at Birmingham. A major concern of hers since the mid-1960s has been the conceptualization of goals and objectives for early childhood education on the basis of scientific research about children's development of knowledge. Convinced that the only theory in existence that explains this development from infancy to adolescence was that of Jean Piaget, she studied under him as a postdoctoral research fellow and, later, on a joint appointment with the University of Geneva and the University of Illinois at Chicago. She has been working closely with teachers for 20 years to develop practical ways of using Piaget's constructivist theory in the classroom.

Otis Baker is Assistant Commissioner of Education in the Missouri Department of Elementary and Secondary Education. He was formerly a secondary teacher, principal, and Director of Chapter 1 Programs in the Missouri state department of education.

Linda Barber is a kindergarten teacher at Goshen Elementary School in the Springfield Public School District in Oregon. She has taught kindergarten and first grade for seven years and fourth and fifth grades for four years. She is also a student in a doctoral program in curriculum and instruction at the University of Oregon.

Christine Chaillé is Associate Professor of Teacher Education at the University of Oregon, where she also serves as Coordinator of Elementary Education and as Director of the Early Childhood Center, the laboratory school for the graduate program in Early Childhood Education.

Anne G. Dorsey is Associate Professor and Coordinator of Early Childhood Education at the University of Cincinnati. She has served as president of the National Association of Early Childhood Teacher Educators and is a member of the Ethics Commission of the National Association for the Education of Young Children and of the Early Childhood Education Commission, Association of Teacher Educators.

Brenda S. Engel is Associate Professor in the Division of Advanced Graduate Study and Research, Lesley College Graduate School, in Cambridge, Massachusetts. Her field is qualitative evaluation with a special interest in literacy learning in the primary grades.

Shirley P. Grover is Superintendent of Schools of the Scarborough School Department in Maine. She was formerly Deputy Superintendent of Schools in South Portland after serving as Curriculum Coordinator in the same school department. She has also been an assistant superintendent, a junior high school principal, and an elementary and junior high school teacher in various school districts in Maine.

Susan Harman is Project Director of the American Reading Council and a family therapist in private practice. She was the psychologist at the Central Park East Schools in the New York City public school system for seven years.

Mieko Kamii is Assistant Professor of Psychology at Wheelock College in Boston, where she is helping future teachers understand how children develop. Her research interest is in children's cognitive development related to mathematics.

Steven J. Leinwand is Mathematics Consultant in the Connecticut Department of Education. He is a member of the Mathematical Sciences Education Board and serves on the Board of Directors of the National Council of Supervisors of Mathematics. He was formerly an officer of the Association of State Supervisors of Mathematics.

Dode Morgan-Worsham is Principal of Ruth Fyfe Elementary School in Las Vegas, Nevada. She was formerly Kindergarten Consultant for the Clark County School District in Nevada and is a doctoral student in early childhood education at the University of Alabama at Birmingham.

Deborah Murphy was Director of Early Childhood Education of the Missouri Department of Elementary and Secondary Education until recently and is now Principal of Maplewood Elementary School in North Kansas City, Missouri. She is also a doctoral student in educational administration at the University of Missouri, Columbia.

Vito Perrone is Senior Lecturer, Director of the Teacher Education Programs, and Chair of the Teaching, Curriculum, and Learning Environments Program at Harvard University. He is also Senior Fellow at the Carnegie Foundation for the Advancement of Teaching and has been Convener of the North Dakota Study Group for Evaluation since 1972.

Vasha Rosenblum is Enrichment Specialist in the Hoover City Schools in Alabama. She has taught gifted children in grades K–8 for seven years and is a doctoral student in early childhood education at the University of Alabama at Birmingham.

Eugene W. Thompson is Chair of the Department of Educational Administration and Supervision at Bowling Green State University. He was formerly Deputy Superintendent of the Anchorage School District in Alaska and Superintendent of the Manchester Community Schools in Michigan. He has held several administrative positions in curriculum and evaluation in addition to serving as an elementary school principal.

Introduction:
Rethinking Assessment
and Education

American education has been on a bandwagon again. This time it is the "let's-get-higher-test-scores" bandwagon. Like other quick fixes, the raising-test-scores solution gives the appearance of improving education but creates hosts of new problems.

Test scores are rising in the United States because grown-ups in various positions, with good intentions, are playing games without realizing the damage they are doing. Among the games being played are the vote-getting game, the looking-good game, the keep-my-job game, and the buck-passing game.

The vote-getting game is played by legislators, governors, and board of education members at the state and local levels. Politicians know they can get votes by promising greater educational accountability. These promises, usually carried out by imposing more testing, are popular because they are simple to put into effect: Give students tests to see if they are learning, and do not pass them unless they perform at a level considered good enough to promote them to the next level. Demands for testing and accountability work so well in politicians' favor that all 50 states now have mandates requiring schools to give tests.

Many elected officials cannot be expected to know early childhood education or the inadequacy of standardized achievement tests for evaluating young children's learning. Educators should know these things, however, and the games educators play are difficult to defend.

As Eugene W. Thompson and Steven J. Leinwand describe in Chapters 3 and 8 respectively, the process most often begins with superintendents. Responding to policies set by their boards of education, superintendents put pressure on others as they pass the "let's-get-those-test-scores-up" message down the line.

The looking-good game is influenced by the fact that test scores are published in newspapers; comparisons among schools and districts make great news. While mandates require only that tests be given, the looking-good game transforms these mandates into requirements to produce ever higher test scores. Superintendents understandably want their districts to look good; principals likewise feel compelled to present their schools in the most favorable light; and teachers consequently feel the daily pressure for higher test scores. The pressures engendered by the looking-good game are so great that by 1987 the average test scores of all 50 states were found to be above the national average (Cannell, 1987; Baker, Burstein, Linn, & Shepard, 1989)! This peculiar phenomenon has occurred because educators have responded to pressures for higher test scores by teaching the tests or teaching to the tests. Since the norms of standardized achievement tests are established before they are published, it is possible for the average test scores of all 50 states to be above the national average in subsequent years.

More intense than the looking-good game is the keep-my-job game. In some situations superintendents fear the loss of their jobs unless they produce higher test scores. For principals and teachers, the keep-my-job game concerns teaching methods and materials. Worksheets, drill, and certain programs are known to produce higher test scores, and some principals check up on teachers daily to ensure that the prescribed number of worksheets has been completed, regardless of how mindless or inappropriate they may be. Too often we hear complaints about principals who demand that teachers get students ready for the tests with weeks of worksheet drill. Principals, too, are often forced to compromise their own beliefs. While it is true that people have to make a living, one wonders if it is necessary for so many educators to silence their professional consciences to earn their paychecks.

Among measurement specialists and testing coordinators in state departments of education and local school systems, the keep-my-job game results not only in more testing but also in the buck-passing game. These specialists know that their testing programs result in drill focusing on superficial questions and answers, but some of them say that if teachers are misusing the test, the responsibility lies with the teachers, not the evaluators. Few state and local testing coordinators feel an obligation to speak up against tests that result in drill and practice of superficial academic skills.

Some educators and policymakers have become sufficiently disturbed by this state of affairs that they are beginning to ask questions about the outcomes of our games. In a report entitled *Right From the Start* about 4- to 8-year-olds, the National Association of State Boards of Education (1988) took a surprisingly strong stand with ground-breaking statements such as the following:

> . . . Preschool, kindergarten and primary grade teachers report an increasing use of standardized tests, worksheets and workbooks, ability grouping, retention and other practices that focus on academic skills too early and in inappropriate ways.
>
> . . . Policies have been adopted that, while perhaps appropriate for improving high schools, may be less helpful for elementary schools and very young children. For example, it may well be the case that making high school students work harder is an appropriate formulation. However, lack of effort is not the problem for kindergarten students.
>
> The legitimate concern about the link between our economic future and the quality of schooling has fostered a competitive mentality for our educational enterprise, with unfortunate consequences for early segments of schooling. If education is seen as a contest that pits children against their peers, or a race against our foreign competitors, we risk teaching very young children the wrong academic tasks in an inappropriate fashion before they are ready, and we stimulate fears and pressure among parents.
>
> . . . Thinking in young children is directly tied to their interactions with people and materials. Young children learn best and most by actively exploring their environment, using hands-on materials and building upon their natural curiosity and desire to make sense of the world around them. (pp. 3–5)

Other national organizations such as the Association for Childhood Education International (Perrone, 1977), the Association for Supervision and Curriculum Development (1987), the National Association for the Education of Young Children (1988a), the National Association of Early Childhood Teacher Educators

(1989), the National Association of Elementary School Principals (1989), the National Council of Teachers of English (1989), and the National Council of Teachers of Mathematics (1989) have made similar statements calling for an end to drilling children on isolated skills, which achievement testing encourages.

The purpose of this volume is to persuade the reader to join in the swelling effort, led by thoughtful leaders including parents, to call a halt to achievement testing in grades K–2, and to rethink not only assessment procedures but also our educational goals and methods of teaching.

The authors of this book are not against accountability. We are all for it. Our reasons for opposing the use of achievement tests are that they are not valid measures of accountability and that they are producing classroom practices harmful to young children's development.

Although this book is about achievement testing, our concerns apply also to "readiness" tests. "Readiness" tests such as the Gesell School Readiness Test (Gesell Institute of Human Development, 1980) and the Brigance K and 1 Screen for Kindergarten and First Grade (Brigance, 1982) have the same effects as achievement tests. They encourage teachers to adjust their teaching to match what is on the tests, just as norm-referenced achievement tests do. Tests originally intended to serve educational programs thus end up dictating them, resulting in "a narrowing of the curriculum, a concentration on those skills most amenable to testing, a constraint on the creativity and flexibility of teachers, and a demeaning of teachers' professional judgment" (Meisels, 1989, p. 17).

Many educators and policymakers say that they would be willing to give up achievement tests if better instruments were offered as replacements. It is not the purpose of this book to offer alternative instruments. Before alternative instruments can be developed or used, it is necessary to conceptualize goals and objectives that can be justified on the basis of what we now know about how children learn. Are we trying to achieve short-term objectives that are easy to teach and easy to measure? What is the relationship between surface skills (such as ability to count) and deeper, general abilities (such as the logic of addition and of knowing that $3 + 6 = 6 + 3$)? What is the relationship between short-term objectives (such as knowledge of consonants and vowels) and long-term goals (such as ability to read critically or with enjoyment)? Are sociomoral goals relevant to education and accountability? What is the relationship between early childhood education and the drug problem, the drop-out problem, and teen-age pregnancies? As we will see in Chapter 9, the task force appointed by the Missouri Commissioner of Education addressed these questions about goals in depth before it began work on assessment. If our goals and objectives are not based on sound, scientific theory about how children learn in depth, demonstrating progress toward them is of little value.

Unless educators and policymakers understand the interplay of grown-ups' games, the use of new assessment tools will result only in another looking-good game. For example, the inventory Brenda Engel recommends in Chapter 11 was made on the assumption that the teacher using it is trying to foster the development of literacy from within the child. Unless the intent of a new tool is clearly understood, merely switching instruments could mean jumping out of one frying pan into another.

This book is intended for a variety of audiences: educators, parents, legislators and other elected and appointed officials, school board members, members of the press, and voters in general. Because we wanted to address many audiences, we limited technical terms and references as much as possible. More than any other group, teachers are frustrated because they *know* that achievement tests are inadequate, but they are not sure enough of their arguments to speak up against these tests. This book was written especially with these teachers in mind so that they will be able to articulate the reasons for their conviction.

Chapter 1 begins with a sketch of how we got into the present state of affairs. Vito Perrone, a long-time opponent of the use of standardized tests for evaluation, and convener of the North Dakota Study Group on Evaluation since 1972, explains in this chapter some terms and concepts used in test construction. In Chapter 2, Mieko Kamii and I explain why achievement tests are not valid measures of learning, how they promote classroom practices that are harmful to young children's development, and why the authors of this book are calling for a halt to achievement testing in grades K–2.

Chapters 3 through 9 were written from the perspectives of superintendents (Chapter 3 by Eugene W. Thompson), principals (Chapter 5 by Dode Morgan-Worsham), teachers (Chapter 6 by Christine Chaillé and Linda Barber), teacher educators (Chapter 7 by Anne G. Dorsey), and consultants in state departments of education (Chapter 8 by Steven J. Leinwand). Policymakers and the public will probably be surprised to learn how the pressure for higher test scores works against real improvements in schools. Without an understanding of the games grown-ups play, people will go on asking for illusory "evidence" of gains. Chapters 4 (by Shirley Grover) and 9 (by Deborah Murphy and Otis Baker) were written by exceptionally autonomous leaders who are initiating fundamental changes in a school district and a state department of education, respectively.

Chapters 10 through 13 focus more specifically on literacy development and mathematics. Chapters 10 (by Susan Harman) and 12 (by Mieko Kamii and me) describe the negative effects of achievement testing on how reading, writing, and mathematics are taught. Chapters 11 (by Brenda Engel) and 13 (by Vasha Rosen-blum and me) describe alternative approaches to assessment. These chapters are not intended to be recipes but to illustrate a conception of assessment that can be used by educators who understand how young children learn.

For people who do not have time to read all the chapters, I recommend Chapter 14. This final chapter summarizes the actions that educators can take and suggests ways to inform and influence parents, policymakers, the media, and voters in general.

The final message is that time and money would be better spent on rethinking our goals in a fundamental way and improving the preservice and in-service education of teachers and administrators than on all this excessive, ill-advised testing. Putting pressure on school people to raise test scores is like telling football coaches to win at all costs. When winning becomes all-important, students' education and physical and emotional well-being are often sacrificed. When test scores become all-important, young children's development is likewise sacrificed in the name of excellence. We hope the ideas presented in this book will help educators, policymakers, and the public rethink what schools ought to be doing for young children and move in a different direction. A narrow, superficial focus on academic skills that overlooks young children's social, moral, intellectual, and motivational development is undesirable for them as individuals and for the future of our country.

Constance Kamii
Birmingham, Alabama
September 1989

Chapter 1

How Did We Get Here?

Vito Perrone

Standardized tests exist in American society for almost every human trait imaginable, from intelligence and achievement to alienation, self-concept to maturity, moral development to creativity. While these tests have come to affect Americans of all ages, in all fields, intelligence and achievement tests come down most heavily on the young, those between the ages of 3 and 21. Although problematic for young people at all ages and levels of schooling, they are particularly deleterious for children in preschools and primary grades. For it is in these early years that children's growth is so uneven, so idiosyncratic, that large numbers of skills needed for success in school are in such fluid acquisitional stages.

I cry when I read about young children "held back" on the basis of a test, or placed in one or another of the schooling tracks that support various judgments about children's potential. And I wonder about those who believe that testing young children and then making place-ment, promotion, or retention decisions on the basis of such testing leads to any constructive ends. Such decisions are not founded on any significant body of research (Shepard, 1987). They certainly don't follow from any knowledge of young children rooted in close observa-tion and a high level of personal investment in their well-being.

Sheldon White, a Harvard psychologist, suggests that in regard to standardized tests we are contending with "an affair in which magic, science and myth are intermixed" (White, 1975, p. 10). He may well be offering an understatement! How many of us, for example, actually believe that the intelligence and competence of an individual can be adequately represented by *any* of the standardized tests given in our schools? Or that there is *one* distribution curve—whatever the metric —capable of classifying all children? Or that a particular score on a test can provide a genuinely defensible demarcation between those who should be promoted to the next grade level and those who should be retained, those who need help and those who don't? Such assumptions defy almost everything we have come to understand about children's growth as well as their responses to particular educational encounters.

Even if one fails to take note of the implicit assumptions of the tests, essentially that the knowledge or competence of children *can be measured* by the number of correct answers they supply, examination of the test items and the composition of the tests (something those in schools do too little of) ought to cause some measure of pause, if not enormous concern.

- Are the questions clear?
- Do they address the particular educational concerns of teachers? of parents?
- Do the tests as a whole provide useful information about individual children? about a class?
- Do they support children's intentions as learners?
- Do they provide *essential* information to children's parents?

In all of my years of working with teachers and parents, I have encountered few able to provide an affirmative answer to *any* of the foregoing questions. That teachers and parents can offer so little positive response is surely suggestive of problems with the tests and the emphasis given to them.

In contrast, however, almost all teachers tend to respond affirmatively to the following questions:

- Do you feel any pressure to teach to the tests?
- If the tests were not given or used for the evaluation of individual children, teachers, and schools, would you use fewer skill sheets and workbooks and other simple-response pedagogical materials?
- Would you use a broader range of instructional materials, and give more attention to integrated learning?
- Would expectations for *all* children enlarge?
- Would you devote more attention to process-oriented mathematics and science and to the arts?
- Would the curriculum be more powerful, more generative?
- Do you feel that you can assess children's learning in more appropriate ways than through the use of standardized achievement tests?

Such responses need to be given more serious attention.

Used as they are in many settings for major educational decisions, the various tests clearly limit the educational possibilities for children. We need to understand this well, for the pressures to use more tests for more purposes continue to grow.

A historical perspective

Although examinations of student knowledge have long existed in and around schools, the standardized achievement and aptitude testing that currently prevails is a 20th Century phenomenon. The *Thorndike Handwriting Scale*, produced in 1909, was the first popular standardized achievement test used in the public schools. A wide variety of achievement and aptitude tests quickly followed. By the 1930s a majority of schools across the country were engaged in some form of standardized testing, but the scope was *extremely* small by today's standards. Few people who completed high school before 1950 took more than three standardized tests in their entire school careers. The results of such tests were hardly ever discussed. Parents didn't receive the scores, and school-wide results certainly never appeared in newspapers.

By contrast, students who completed high school in 1989 took 18 to 21 standardized tests during their school careers. To understand the magnitude of the shift, note that since 1950 the volume of testing has grown at the annual rate of 10 to 20% (Haney & Madaus, 1989). Moreover, 1989 graduates, rather than taking the tests matter-of-factly, as had students prior to 1950, most likely paid considerable attention to preparation for them, spending many days on practice tests. They probably heard admonitions about "doing your best" and "how important this test is to you and to our school." Further, the test scores of these 1989 graduates have, over the years, filled many pages of the newspapers and been the "talk of the town." Test scores, especially if they are high, have even become a central element in the arsenal of real estate brokers: When people with school-age children are house hunting, they are simultaneously looking for schools, so may be influenced by test scores whether or not the scores prove anything about the quality of the schools.

Those not familiar with contemporary practices in schools would be surprised at how much time is actually spent on test preparation. During these test preparation periods, reading often ceases being a matter of real books, writing that matters ends, math stops having a connection to the world, and the arts, it they exist at all, are shelved. Primary teachers I have discussed this with are not pleased about what they are providing children, even as their children are scoring better each year on the tests.

In regard to press accounts, I still have vividly engraved in my memory a recent headline in the *Minneapolis Tribune*: "Minneapolis Holds Back 11% of its Kindergartners." The story didn't report that a disproportionate number of those held back *on the basis of the kindergarten test* were from poor and minority families, or that the decisions very likely guaranteed much more failure for these children than success (Shepard, 1987).

Another measure of the changes in testing is instructive. Testing practices, as noted earlier, began an upward spiral after 1950. Tests were used increasingly more often for selection and retention purposes. Still, at least up to 1965, they would have to be seen as relatively benign by today's standards. In addition, prior to 1965, the tests were not often used in the early grades. This is important to understand. There was consensus associated with the traditions that gave rise to the kindergarten, as well as to the subsequent developmental beliefs guiding the primary grades as a whole, that the early years were "special," a time for natural growth and development. Where serious testing programs existed, they generally began in third or fourth grade.

Testing, however, exploded after 1965, especially with regard to its uses. As evaluation demands grew with the influx of new federal and state resources for schools, the tests were quickly seen as inexpensive and easy measures for meeting these demands. With the accountability movement of the 1970s, the tests quickly became the definers of standards in almost all curriculum areas.

By the mid-1970s, testing started to regularly invade the primary grades. Earlier developmental understandings began to erode, and people who continued to teach in developmentally appropriate ways and to treat tests lightly became an unhappy minority. Early years testing became a growing area.

The overall level of testing took another major leap "forward" after the publication of *A Nation at Risk* (National Commission on Excellence in Education, 1983) as governors and legislators initiated new and more extensive testing programs. The expansion included the early years. Increasingly, tests are being used to determine children's readiness to enter, and to leave, kindergarten. They are also being used extensively

Testing practices began an upward spiral after 1950. Tests were used increasingly more often for selection and retention purposes. Still, at least up to 1965, they would have to be seen as relatively benign by today's standards. In addition, prior to 1965, the tests were not often used in the early grades. This is important to understand. There was a consensus associated with the traditions that gave rise to the kindergarten, as well as to the subsequent developmental beliefs guiding the primary grades as a whole, that the early years were "special," a time for natural growth and development. Where serious testing programs existed, they generally began in third or fourth grade.

for placement decisions, essentially early tracking (National Association for the Education of Young Children, 1988a; Bredekamp & Shepard, 1989). It is time to make children's learning the focus of our attention, and the tests have almost nothing to do with learning.

The technical aspects of the tests

This book will provide readers with a number of powerful arguments about the need to end early years testing. In the process, it raises issues and discusses problems in the fabric of standardized tests themselves. To make the latter understandable, I will devote some attention to the technical aspects of the tests in order to demystify the scientism that surrounds testing. I do so because those who advocate more sensible and responsible approaches to getting close to children's learning typically confront the scientism and, lacking enough technical understanding to engage in productive dialogue, are too often placed on the defensive. In discussions of standardized testing, one often finds such terms as *objectivity, standardization, reliability*, and *validity*. All carry the aura of science, but in fact they are scientific only about superficial aspects of human learning. What do these terms mean in nontechnical language? My focus here is on norm-referenced tests because their use is more extensive than criterion-referenced tests.

Objectivity. A test is considered objective if everyone takes it under the same conditions. The multiple choice format, buttressed by a single right answer pattern, supports this basic definition of objectivity. But objectivity has nothing to do with whether a test is fair, contains items of importance, or has ambiguous questions and answers. Objectivity has, in other words, *no particular relationship to quality.*

Standardization. A test is standardized if norms or specific scoring metrics have been established. Whether the norm populations are representative in more than a statistical sense, however, is not the defining characteristic. This term, as in the case for objectivity, *has no relationship to quality.*

Reliability. Reliability relates to the consistency of the test: How close, for example, are the results for an individual or group at two different testings? Or, how close are the scores of individuals on two different forms of a particular test? Reliability is rather simple to establish. A test can have very high reliability (most popular standardized achievement tests carry reliability coefficients of .87 to .93) and yet be a very poor test, measuring little considered important to large numbers of people who use or take the test. The latter point relates to validity, a subject which doesn't receive very much attention.

Validity. At the most simple level, validity refers to the degree to which a test measures what it is supposed to measure and/or the degree to which the scores derived from a particular test can be related to what the test is supposed to be measuring. In other words, what are the inferences that can be drawn from the test scores? A close examination of a number of reading tests, for example, provides convincing evidence that they are *not* about reading. Many tests that purport to be about writing do not ask students to do any writing. Such tests pose serious validity problems.

Among all these technical formulations, validity is the *most* important. Yet, it is given the *least* attention. Unlike reliability, validity is difficult to establish with any authority.

Validity is typically determined by having an expert (or experts) examine a particular test and provide the equivalent of an imprimatur. This is content validation by opinion and is the focus of most standardized tests used in the schools. (Those who suggest, for example, that the tests contain a racial or socioeconomic bias are, in essence, questioning content validity by claiming that the test content is not representative of the socioeducational experience of minority people.) Validity is also established by comparing the test results with other measures (i.e., other tests, grades, or teacher judgments). In the psychometric field, this process is called face validity. A claim that a particular test has face validity doesn't necessarily mean, however, that the test addresses significantly the subject under consideration.

Test content and construction

So much for the terms. What can be said about test content? For many individuals with reservations about standardized tests, the content is the principal issue. This relates to the concept of validity but is, at the same time, broader. The currently most used standardized achievement tests have been constructed to conform to instructional programs, with predetermined objectives and materials, through which everyone is expected to work. Such programs tend to give primary attention to information and little encouragement to serious thought. The tests have less relationship to programs that stress high levels of individualization and flexibility of objectives, matters which typically relate to higher order thought.

In recent years, the public has become concerned because scores have increased so quickly—they are now above average in almost all communities and states; yet on activities emphasizing application and "higher order thought," the results are discouraging. We shouldn't be surprised. The increase in scores suggests that the schools have become increasingly more successful in teaching the low level skills demanded by the tests.

How are the tests constructed? In preparing items for an achievement test, authors typically survey the basal materials commonly used in schools; they also attempt to learn about the sequence, if any, that tends to exist in various content/subject areas; and they make decisions about how to establish a balance between information items and concept items. Given the multiple choice technology, however, information items are easier to develop. Questions are prepared and tried out in a variety of school settings. (The particular items selected to try out represent, in effect, a statement about what the test authors consider important. This is not intended as a negative observation; it is, however, a condition we need to understand.) Those items that most individuals get right or wrong are discarded. *Distribution* is desired, inasmuch as the entire battery of items is designed to produce, among a sample of students who take the test, a *normal curve*, that is, a construct in which half the students score below the average and half above. In such a process, items that many would suggest are important might well be discarded and items of limited importance retained.

Teachers, school administrators, and parents would do well to examine closely the questions that appear in the standardized tests used in their schools, or being considered for use, in order to make a judgment about the importance of the questions and their relationship to the local curriculum or their largest hopes for curriculum. Assuming we were truly interested in a child's understanding of trees, for example, would we really ask: Which of the following trees grows in the New England states? (a) Rubber tree; (b) Palm tree; (c) Oak tree; (c) Redwood tree. That is the testmaker's approach, but teachers and parents could find many more interesting and appropriate ways to obtain a fuller picture of the child's knowledge. The knowledge parents and teachers would gain from their own constructions would also help them with their continuing nurturance of a child's learning.

Once the items are developed, standardization procedures begin. This involves establishing a norm population and constructing norm scores. (And given the increasing diversity of America's school-age population, finding a norm population is becoming more complex.) How long does all of this take? From start-up to publication, five to eight years might pass. But what if curriculum changes are rapid and/or new goals emerge in schools? Might there then be a gap between the curricular assumptions of the tests and the curricula that actually exist? This has, over the years, been the case. What if teachers really believed that a shift in educatonal direction was necessary? This is the problem discussed by Leinwand in Chapter 8.

The statistics of testing

In addition to the technical aspects of the tests, it is also important to understand test statistics—the derivations that result in particular scores. My experience is that far too few of those who work with and around the tests have much understanding of the scoring mechanisms. Even if the test manuals accompanying standardized tests are replete with information about derived scores—how to interpret them and what limitations need to be taken into account when using them—the manuals are not often available in schools for teachers to read. In fact, what advantage would there be for pressured, hurried teachers to study test manuals if, in the end, they are still required to give the tests and if, in the end, "the system" uses the test scores for its own purposes, regardless of teacher judgments? Further, little information about derived scores goes out to the public to increase their understanding.

Test results are most often reported as percentile scores, stanine scores, or grade-level equivalency scores. Forty-three correct answers out of 80 items on a particular achievement test given to sixth graders converts to a *percentile* score of 52. This indicates that 52% of those who took the test as part of the norm population scored 43 or less, and 48% scored higher than 43. (Tests given to primary children possess the same statistical features.)

Stanine scores, unlike percentile scores and grade-equivalency scores, are suggestive of a range. The diagram on page 10 presents a range of the raw scores on the foregoing test converted to percentiles and then to a stanine scale.

Stanine	1	2	3	4	5	6	7	8	9
Percentile	1-3	4-10	11-22	23-39	40-58	59-76	77-88	89-94	95-99
Raw Score	14-17	18-22	23-28	29-36	37-46	47-55	56-63	64-68	69-80

All raw and percentile scores, for example, are grouped to make up a nine-point, or stanine, scale. A stanine score of 5 is average; 40% of the scores will then fall above this average and 40% below. The percentile score of 52 cited above falls within the fifth stanine, along with all percentile scores between 40 and 58.

The *grade-level equivalency* score is derived essentially by assigning to the median score of a norm population a *grade-level equivalency*. The median for a test given to third graders would be 3.0. Scores above and below the median are then assigned grade-level equivalencies above and below 3.0. It is a matter of estimation, nothing more. (Tests given in kindergarten and grade one use various *primer* designations for grade levels below one.) The raw score of 43 discussed above converts to a percentile score of 52 and a grade-level equivalency of 7.8 (i.e., seventh grade, eight months). A raw score of 45 converts to a percentile score of 56 and a grade-level equivalency score 8.7. *Two questions right or wrong brings a difference of 11 months* (though it doesn't alter the stanine score).

The publisher of the foregoing test lists a *standard error* as 3.9. This standard error indicates that two-thirds of the time one could expect a fluctuation in raw score of up to 3.9. As the test manual notes, "We could expect with about 68% certainty that the true score [for a student with a raw score of 43] would fall between [39 and 47]." This is between the 44th and the 59th percentiles; the grade-level equivalency range for these percentile scores is 7.2 to 8.9 respectively. And one-third of the time there may be even more error. The point of all of this is that *the scores are very imprecise; one should be very careful in attaching too much importance to them.* Yet, they are often treated as weights on a scale.

Of all the derived scores, grade-level equivalency is the most commonly used, even though it is the most misleading. Test publishers now regularly point out in their manuals that grade equivalents are not an equal-unit scale and are not appropriate for interpreting the test performance of individuals and groups. In some cases they even admonish users not to report grade-level equivalencies at all.

Henry Dyer, a highly respected authority in testing, has called grade-level equivalency scores "absurd, wrong, and misleading." In even stronger language he commented in *The United Teacher* (April 14, 1971, p. 15) that they are "statistical monstrosities...[that] lure educational practitioners to succumb to what Alfred North Whitehead called the 'fallacy of misplaced concreteness.'" But grade-level equivalencies continue, in part because school people faced with accountability pressures have been lured to measure *growth* (or "misplaced concreteness"). If children are in school for eight months, the misplaced belief is that they should make eight months' gain. Only grade-level equivalency scores report in grade-month terms. In order to address the question of eight months' growth, of course, one has to assume that growth is unidimensional and linear and that eight months of schooling corresponds empirically with eight months' gain on a standardized test. Neither is the case.

Of all the derived scores, grade-level equivalency is the most commonly used, even though it is the most misleading. Test publishers now regularly point out in their manuals that grade equivalents are not an equal-unit scale and are not appropriate for interpreting the test performance of individuals and groups. In some cases they even admonish users not to report grade-level equivalencies at all. Henry Dyer, a highly respected authority in testing, has called grade-level equivalency scores "absurd, wrong, and misleading."

What does it mean to be told that a second grade child (or class) is reading at a "6.9 grade level"? Does it suggest, as I have often heard or read in the newspapers, that this particular child (or class) is reading as well as average-achieving children completing the sixth grade? What the tests measure as reading ability in second grade is not necessarily the same thing as the reading ability measured in the sixth grade. A score of 6.9 is nothing more than an extrapolation above the mean. It has in no real sense *anything* to do with how well a child completing the sixth grade reads. Conversely, if a sixth grader has a grade-level equivalency score of 4.0 on a reading test designed for sixth graders, this does not mean that the child reads only as well as a fourth grader. The chances are that if this sixth grader took the test designed for fourth graders, his grade-level equivalency score might be 6.0. We need to remember that the tests were normed at particular grade levels. Second graders don't take a test designed for sixth graders and sixth graders don't take a test designed for fourth graders. We are contending solely with a statistical construct. Yet the use of grade-level equivalency scores goes on unabated.

Beyond the technical issues

Much of this technical discussion has dealt with test scores in a broad sense. The problems, however, grow as the context narrows and the tests are used to say something about an individual child's achievement of particular skills or to determine specific instructional needs. Given the content sampling involved, the manner in which the tests have been constructed, the paper-and-pencil multiple choice format, and the sources that exist for error, using the tests as a basis for judging children or guiding their instruction isn't a particularly valid use, even though such a justification often accompanies decisions to use the tests.

In order to make decisions about individuals, individual student scores on subparts or responses to specific test items must be used. Even from a technical perspective this is a significant problem. The sources of error are large. For example, the health of a child on the day the test is given can affect the score. Noise in the classroom, teacher attitudes toward the test, whether a child has taken similar tests, a broken pencil, and any number of similar disturbances can influence a particular score. The mental state of a child—boredom, elation, anxiety about the test—can also make a difference in how she or he performs. In addition, simple mechanical errors such as marking the wrong box on the test sheet by accident, overlooking a question, or missing a word while reading are relatively common test-taking problems. Thus a child's real knowledge and understandings on the occasion of this single exercise may be considerably underestimated.

Many of the sources of difficulty outlined above—and the surface has scarcely been scratched—can affect an individual's score. Such sources of difficulty have little to do with how "good" the test is, how carefully it was prepared, or the validity of its content. These difficulties are, in general, intrinsic to the nature of standardized testing.

How serious are all of these difficulties? It depends to a large degree, of course, on how the test results are used. In reports of test scores for large groups of children, we can expect that many of the mechanical errors and related difficulties suggested above will balance out; some children will score above their "true" knowledge or skill level by chance, and others below. The larger the group tested, the more likely that such a balancing will occur. For a single individual, however, no other score exists. Nothing can compensate for error when a single score for an individual is used for such purposes as curriculum placement, advancement, and the like.

Conclusion

In this chapter, I have provided a context for this volume: a history of the testing practices that we have allowed to get a stranglehold on the schools; and an entry into the technical aspects of the tests, their scoring mechanisms and problems. Teachers and parents have been told that the tests have meaning, that they point out what children know and understand, that they can help give important direction to instruction. The tests *don't* match that promise. Their contribution to the education of young children is virtually nil. The education of young children will not be filled with large possibilities and equity will not become paramount if these tests continue to play such a big role. The tyranny of these tests needs to end.

Chapter 2

Why Achievement Testing Should Stop

Constance Kamii and Mieko Kamii

The authors of this book are calling for a halt to achievement testing in grades K–2 for two reasons: These tests are not valid measures of children's learning or of teachers' accountability, and the pressure for higher test scores is resulting in classroom practices that are harmful to young children's development. To explain this statement, we need to discuss how young children acquire knowledge and moral values. After describing the process of acquisition, we will show how different theories about development and learning lead to different kinds of goals and objectives for instruction, different methods of teaching, and different approaches to the evaluation of outcomes.

How children acquire knowledge and moral values

According to traditional assumptions, children acquire knowledge and moral values by internalizing them from the environment. However, Jean Piaget and his collaborators amply demonstrated with more than 60 years of research that children acquire knowledge and moral values by constructing them from the inside, in interaction with the environment, rather than by internalizing them directly from the environment. Examples of children's acquisition of spoken language, written language, number concepts, and moral values will illustrate this theory, called constructivism.

Spoken language

Most American children learn to speak English, and most French children learn to speak French. It is, therefore, easy to think that children learn languages by internalizing them from the environment.

A closer look, however, leads us to another conclusion. Babies first utter single words such as "Ba-a!" (ball) in spite of the fact that no one in their environment talks in this way. They later say more than one word such as "Ball gone" and "Daddy sock," and produce utterances such as "Markie me pushed," "My foots hurt," and "I thinked it in my head."

Children cannot be said to have learned any of these expressions by direct internalization from the environment because no one in the environment talks in these ways. Young children all over the world learn to talk by constructing one level after another of "wrong" forms of their native speech. This is particularly clear when they have constructed grammatical rules for forming plurals ("my foots") or the past tense ("I thinked"). Children do not learn by internalizing knowledge in ready-made form. They acquire it by constructing one level after another of "wrong" forms of knowledge.

Written language

Based on research conducted by Ferreiro and Teberosky (1979/1982) with Spanish-speaking children in Argentina, Manning, Long, Manning, and Kamii (1987) studied the development of spelling in English-speaking kindergartners in the United States. The developmental levels found were strikingly similar to those reported for Argentinian youngsters. When asked in individual interviews to write various words, level-1 children produced strings of letters such as "BtyterilGloriLi" when asked to write *vacation,* "JterithG" when asked to write *motion,* and "teritLLGlorWVnL" for *ocean.*

At the second level, the kindergartners wrote words with a fixed quantity (such as four) or a minimum and maximum number of letters. For example, one level-2 child wrote "VWGEE" for *vacation,* "OMGE" for *motion,* "VSA" for *vale/veil,* and "OEILE" for *ocean,* thus behaving as if there were a rule stating that words are written with a minimum of three and a maximum of five letters. Children cannot be said to have internalized such a rule because there is no rule in English or Spanish stating that all words have to be written with a minimum of three and a maximum of five letters. (This particular child also wrote most of the conventional first letters of the words.)

At the third level, kindergartners wrote such letters as "VKN" for *vacation,* "MON" for *motion,* "VL" for *vale/veil,* and "OEN" for *ocean.* Systematic sound-letter correspondences appear for the first time at this level, beginning mostly with consonants. The title of Bissex's

(1980) book *GYNS AT WRK (Genius at Work)* is another example of level-3 writing.

Vowels appear systematically at level 4, as can be seen in "VACA-SHUN," "MOSHUN," "VAL," and "OSHUN." Children's construction of spelling has come to be widely known as "invented spelling" and once again demonstrates how children construct their own systems, one after another, rather than internalizing the correct, adult system in a ready-made form. Similar research conducted in Brazil, Israel, Italy, Mexico, and Switzerland has also demonstrated that children construct one "wrong" system of spelling after another (Bamberger, Ferreiro, Frey-Streiff, & Sinclair, 1988).

Number concepts

A young child's construction of number concepts can be demonstrated with a task deveised by Inhelder and Piaget (1963). The child is given one of two identical glasses, and the adult takes the other. Using a collection of small objects (e.g., beads or beans), the adult asks the child to drop one bead into his glass each time she drops one into hers. After five or six beads have been dropped with one-to-one correspondence, the adult says, "Let's stop now, and you watch what I'm going to do ." The adult drops one bead into her glass and then suggests, "Let's get going again." The adult and child drop several more beads into their glasses with one-to-one correspondence until the adult says, "Let's stop." This is what has happened so far:

$$\text{Adult:} \quad 1+1+1+1+1+1+1+1+1+1+1$$
$$\text{Child:} \quad 1+1+1+1+1 \qquad 1+1+1+1+1$$

The adult then asks, "Do we have the same number (or amount), or do *you* have more, or do *I* have more?

Four-year-olds usually reply that the two glasses have the same amount. When asked, "How do you know we have the same amount?" the child explains, "Because I can see that we have the same number." However, some 4-year-olds reply that *they* have more, and when we asked how they know, they simply say, "Because." The adult continues, "Do you remember how we dropped the beads?" and 4-year-olds usually give all the empirical facts correctly: ". . . Then you told me to stop, and you put one in your glass, and I watched 'cause you told me to wait. Then we got going again." Four-year-olds remember all the observable, empirical facts correctly but base their judgment of equality on the empirical appearance of the two quantities.

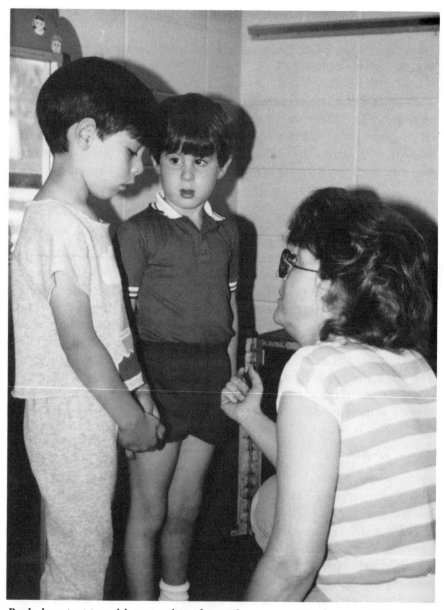

Books by expert practitioners written for teachers or parents of young children often suggest approaches to "discipline problems" and "classroom management" that foster moral development and problem solving on the part of children themselves (Gordon, 1975; Warren, 1977; Stone, 1978; Seefeldt, 1980; Gartrell, 1987; Hendrick, 1988; Greenberg, in press).

By age 5 or 6, however, most children deduce that the adult has one more. When we ask these children how they know, they invoke exactly the same observable facts as the 4-year-olds. Children who gave the correct answer are then asked, "If we continued to drop beads all day in the same way (with one-to-one correspondence), do you think we will have the same number at the end, or will *you* have more, or will *I* have more?" Five- and 6-year-olds divide themselves into two groups. The more advanced children say that there will *always* be one more in the adult's glass, while the others make empirical statements: "I can't know because we haven't done it yet," or "You don't have enough beads to keep going all day."

Adults do not teach children to drop beads into glasses and to say that the adult's glass has one more; yet researchers all over the world have found by giving a variety of tasks that children construct number concepts from the inside. To understand this construction, let us consider the three kinds of knowledge Piaget distinguished according to their ultimate sources and modes of structuring: physical knowledge, logico-mathematical knowledge, and social (conventional) knowledge.

Physical knowledge is knowledge of objects in external reality. The weight of a wooden bead and the knowledge that it falls when we let go of it are examples of physical knowledge that can be acquired through sensory experiences.

Logico-mathematical knowledge, on the other hand, consists of relationships created by each individual. Presented with a red bead and a blue one, we can think about them as being different (in color) or the same (in weight). While the color and weight of the beads are *in* the objects and knowable through sensory experiences, the similarity and difference between them are not. Relationships of similarity and difference are constructed (created mentally) by the individual and imposed on the objects. We can also put the beads into a numerical relationship and think about them as "two." The beads are observable, but the "two-ness" is not. If the child does not put the beads into the relationship "two," the "two-ness" does not exist for him or her. The source of logico-mathematical knowledge is in each child's head, and this is why children all over the world eventually give correct answers in the preceding number task *without* any instruction.

The sources of *social (conventional) knowledge* are conventions made by people. "No jeans at the office," "pay for the goods you take home from the store," and the vocabulary words of the English language are examples of social knowledge. The sources of the words "one, two, three. . ." are people, but the source of the underlying number concepts is in each child's head (logico-mathematical knowledge). Children's acquisition of language, discussed earlier, demonstrates that even social knowledge is acquired by a process of construction from the inside.

Moral rules and values

Piaget (1932/1965) asked children between the ages of 6 and 14 whether it was worse to lie to an adult or to another child. Young children consistently replied that it was worse to lie to an adult. When asked why, they explained that adults can tell when a statement is not true. Older children, by contrast, tended to answer that sometimes one almost *has to* lie to adults, but it is rotten to do it to other children.

These answers again illustrate constructivism. Children are not taught that lies are worse when one is more likely to be caught lying. Yet, they construct these "rules" out of what they have experienced. Fortunately, most go on to construct a higher level of moral reasoning.

Older children's moral reasoning is characterized by increased autonomy — the ability to decide between right and wrong for oneself, by taking relevant factors into account, independently of reward and punishment. Younger children's morality, by contrast, is the morality of heteronomy — being governed by someone else's authority or someone else's rules about right and wrong. For example, when Piaget asked children why it was bad to tell lies, young children explained, "Because you get punished." When he asked, "Would it be all right to lie if you were not punished?" young children replied, "Yes." Children are not taught such moral reasoning, but they construct these rules as they try to make sense of what they experience. Moral rules and values are not acquired by direct internalization from the environment.

Constructivism is very different from traditional assumptions about how children acquire knowledge and moral values. According to traditional assumptions and theories, learning consists of the internalization of knowledge and values transmitted by adults. Traditional assumptions and constructivism (and its close cousins progressive education and developmentally appropriate education) lead to very different ways of defining goals and objectives, different methods of teaching, and different approaches to the evaluation of outcomes. We will now turn to each one of these aspects.

Defining goals and choosing methods of teaching and of evaluation

Goals and objectives

The definition of goals and objectives is central to education because goals and objectives determine *what* will be taught and *how*, and *what* results of instruction will be evaluated and *how*. For example, if children's curiosity and interest in further learning are not explicit goals of teaching, they will be overlooked or ignored both in instruction and in evaluation. Likewise, if critical, independent thinking is not an explicit goal of instruction, it will be excluded from the classroom as well as from measures of accountability.

Curriculum guides vary from state to state but are similar in that they define goals and objectives in a juxtaposed way. Goals for grades K–12 are generally defined in terms of traditional subjects (e.g., language arts and mathematics), general values (e.g., responsibility and citizenship), and specific goals (e.g., drug, sex, and driver education). This way of defining goals is based on the assumption that education consists of putting into children's heads the knowledge, skills, and values we want them to internalize.

Within each subject, curriculum guides also define specific objectives in a juxtaposed way. For example, in beginning reading, ability to name and decode letters comes first; ability to get meaning from words comes later. In primary mathematics, scope-and-sequence charts include: ability to identify a circle, rectangle, square, and triangle; knowledge of inches and centimeters and of pennies, nickels, dimes, and quarters; and ability to tell time to the hour and half-hour. These are juxtaposed narrow, and superficial objectives selected without any justification, based on research about how children learn and develop. Test makers use these kinds of objectives to measure children's achievement.

In contrast, we begin as Piaget (1948/1973) did with autonomy as the broad, long-range goal of education. Autonomy for Piaget is both intellectual and moral. He explained the intellectual aspect in the following way:

> The principal goal of education is to create [people] who are capable of doing new things, not simply of repeating what other generations have done — [people] who are creative, inventive, and discoverers. The second goal of education is to form minds which can be critical,

can verify, and not accept everything they are offered. The great danger today is of slogans, collective opinions, ready-made trends of thought. We have to be able to resist individually, to criticize, to distinguish between what is proven and what is not. So we need pupils who are active, who learn early to find out by themselves, partly by their own spontaneous activity and partly through material we set up for them; who learn early to tell what is verifiable and what is simply the first idea to come to them. (Quoted in Ripple & Rockcastle, 1964, p. 5)

The moral aspect of autonomy parallels intellectual autonomy. Morally autonomous people think independently and critically and make their own decisions about right and wrong by taking relevant factors into account, rather than by following ready-made rules and values. Martin Luther King's struggle for civil rights is an example of moral autonomy. He was governed by what he believed to be morally right.

Within the long-term goal of autonomy, we conceptualize cognitive goals in the context of social, moral, and attitudinal goals. These goals include the following that are necessary for children's development of autonomy:

- Relationships with adults: Children need to form relationships of mutual respect with adults (as opposed to unilateral respect) and to exchange viewpoints with adults.

- Relationships with peers: Children need to respect the rights, ideas, and feelings of other children and to exchange viewpoints with them.

- Relationships to learning: Children need to be curious and creative and to have confidence and initiative.

(Of course, many excellent teachers who have never studied Piaget consider these things essential, too, and teach accordingly day in and day out.)

Undergirding these objectives is a coherent and scientific theory of how autonomy develops. Relationships of mutual respect with adults and peers are necessary for children's development of moral and intellectual autonomy. For example, adults can punish a child for lying (unilateral respect), or they can refrain from punishing him and, instead, look him in the eye with skepticism and affection and say, "I can't believe you because . . . . I want you to sit down for a while and think about what you need to do if you want me to believe you." The child who is thus encouraged to exchange points of view with mutual respect is more likely, over time, to construct the value of honesty from within than the child who is punished. The one who is punished is reinforced in his heteronomy, but the one who is encouraged to construct a rule from within is given an opportunity to develop autonomy.

Exchange of points of view are also necessary for children's development of intellectual autonomy. For example, many first grade teachers mark a worksheet answer as being wrong when a child writes "$5 + 4 = \underline{\quad 8 \quad}$." However, teachers who want children to develop autonomy refrain from correcting the child and, instead, ask the class if everybody agrees. When children are encouraged to exchange points of view with mutual respect, many correct themselves from within. If other children are not present, the teacher might ask, "How did you get 8?" Children often correct themselves in the process of explaining their procedures. This kind of adult-child interaction with mutual respect, frequently seen in the classrooms of outstanding teachers, also supports children's confidence.

Exchanges of viewpoints among peers are necessary for children's moral development, too. For example, when two children are fighting over a toy, adults often tell them that they must share it. Such an imposition of "correct" behavior results in children's submission to adult power. A much better approach is to say to the children, "Why don't you let me keep the toy until *you two* decide what will be fair to both of you. When *you* decide what *you* want to do, I'll return the toy to you." The children may decide that neither child will have the toy or that they should take turns playing with it. This kind of decision making makes an enormous difference to children's development of moral autonomy. Moral values must be constructed from within, through this kind of social interaction, rather than being imposed on the child in ready-made form.

Attitudes and motivation greatly influence learning. Children who are curious and full of initiative and confidence do not wait to be taught the three Rs (Durkins, 1966; Bissex, 1980; Kamii, 1985, 1989b; Willert & Kamii, 1985). Many teachers are acquainted with children who come from families that encourage autonomy, thinking, creativity, and natural saturation in informal literacy experiences, and whose curiosity and initiative are so encouraged that they seem to learn without being taught. Children's curiosity and initiative can, in fact, be said to be more important than the specific skills they learn, because those who are motivated are bound to acquire knowledge.

In the cognitive realm the constructivist approach is to start with children's interests (curiosity and initiative) rather than with traditional subjects and scope-and-sequence charts. The reason is that interest is a manifestation of mental activity, without which knowledge cannot be constructed. For example, young children like to cook, and making cupcakes involves science, reading, and math. Making puppets is another activity that arouses children's interest and initiative. They can decide what materials they might bring from home to make a puppet (planning and creative thinking); they can collect paper towel tubes and count them to know how many more are needed (arithmetic); they can make reminders to themselves to ask their parents to save things (writing). A skillful teacher figures out how to incorporate subject matter learning in these kinds of natural ways.

The overriding cognitive goal in the constructivist framework is that children *think*. Constructivist teachers encourage children to figure out how to spell words, divide cupcakes, and make the head of a puppet stay on a tube. In arithmetic, too, constructivist teachers encourage children to think to invent their own ways of doing $2 + 3$, $7 + 8$, and $16 + 17$. Getting children to invent their own ways is in sharp contrast with traditional math instruction that makes children follow ready-made procedures (Kamii, 1985, 1989b). The objective of traditional math instruction is mainly to get children to give right answers; the objective of constructivist teaching is to get children to think. If children can think, the right answer is bound to follow eventually.

Constructivists and traditionalists are basically in agreement about the desirability of knowledge and values such as responsibility, honesty, independent thinking, and "saying no to drugs." The differences arise out of their theories about how children acquire these ends. Traditionalists believe that all the desired outcomes must be funneled into children's heads, one by one, and this assumption leads to contradictory goals and objectives. For example, traditional education makes children memorize words and ready-made rules of spelling and arithmetic; yet it hopes to produce independent and creative thinkers. Traditional education also makes children memorize words they do not understand and ideas they do not believe; yet it hopes that children will become critical thinkers. Traditional education makes children obedient and conforming; yet it expects them to stand up against peer pressure and to say no to drugs.

When we start with autonomy as the aim of education, such contradictions are far less likely because we conceptualize all our goals and objectives within one framework. In this conceptualization, it is impossible to think about instruction without thinking about children's development of autonomy. It becomes impossible to make children memorize words and ready-made rules while expecting them to become critical, independent thinkers, or to demand obedience and conformity while expecting them to stand up against peer pressure and to say no to drugs. If we want adults to become autonomous citizens in a democratic society, we must raise them from the beginning to be critical thinkers who can make their own decisions by weighing relevant factors. Further details of autonomy as the aim of education, as opposed to the unintended results of traditional education, can be found in Kamii (1982, 1984, 1985).

Teachers trained in nursery education, or in kindergarten/first grade education before the 1960s, are familiar with processes such as: developing much of the curriculum from children's interests and initiatives; encouraging children to plan, think, and solve problems that crop up in their play and social difficulties and in the math, science, and reading they experience in the course of daily classroom living; expecting that children will participate in classroom management; and guiding children's development with the goal of preparing them to be independent citizens in a democratic society.

Methods of teaching

Traditionalists, who assume that children are like empty vessels, believe that the most efficient way to teach is to transmit knowledge and values to children in the most direct way, rather than wasting time letting them make cupcakes and puppets and fill journals with incorrectly spelled words. They also believe in cutting up knowledge into small pieces that are easy to internalize. They believe that the best way to teach these small parts is through lessons and exercises, reinforcement of correct answers, and/or correction of wrong answers. Scope-and-sequence charts, workbooks, and worksheets all stem from the desire to put bits of knowledge efficiently into children's heads. Most educational computer programs in existence today are electronic worksheets that reinforce correct answers and correct wrong ones.

Constructivists believe in indirect methods of teaching that foster children's social, moral, and intellectual development simultaneously from the inside. In kindergarten, for example, constructivist teachers usually provide for long periods of freely chosen activities such as pretend play, block building, games, reading, painting, drawing, and writing. Free choice is important to constructivists because children choose activities in which they are interested, and interest leads to children's personal engagement. Figuring out how to build a store with blocks is far more intriguing than coloring all the squares on a worksheet. Writing "Don't touch" to make a sign to protect a block construction is much more meaningful to a child than copying "don't" and "won't" 10 times on a worksheet. Even when everyone in the class is required to do the same activity, such as writing and drawing in journals, constructivist teachers give a wide variety of choices. They allow children to write about anything they want to, and to spell words in any way that makes sense to them. Similarly, when everyone is to play math games, children can choose the games that interest them.

Constructivist classrooms are noisier and messier than the ones in which worksheets are used because children who exercise initiative and are excited about their activities move around and talk. Children think more when they can act on objects and see objects' reactions. They also think more when they are encouraged to agree or disagree with each other. Their activities are punctuated with social-moral issues such as "Johnny is cheating" and "Suzie won't let me use the blocks." Constructivist teachers, who always think of classroom activities in the context of autonomy as the long-range goal of education, take time to help children learn to negotiate solutions and to make their own decisions about social-moral issues. Many excellent teachers who have never heard the word *constructivist* fit the description given in these pages; they agree with these goals and use these teaching methods.

Methods of evaluation

As Perrone states in Chapter 1, makers of achievement tests begin by delineating objectives for each subject at each grade level. To determine representative curriculum objectives for each subject at each grade level, test makers analyze the most widely used textbook series, as well as state and large-city curriculum guides and syllabi, and then select objectives common to the greatest number of states. Some examples from spelling, reading, and mathematics in the first two grades illustrate how achievement tests define objectives on the basis of outdated, traditional assumptions about learning.

Spelling. The objectives for makers of achievement tests are correct, adult forms of spelling. As can be seen in the following test item, children are presented with three or four possible choices, only one of which counts as the correct answer.

Some animals eat only at _____.

nit

nite

night

nyte

This test item assumes that children learn to spell by internalizing correct, adult forms of spelling. Achievement tests overlook progress from the level of writing "TOQAC" to that of writing "NIT," or from "NIT" to "NITE." Makers of achievement tests got their objectives from textbooks and curriculum guides written by people who either did not know or did not care that children progress from one level after another of being "wrong."

Reading. Makers of achievement tests think of beginning reading as the decoding of written signs into sounds. Objectives for reading are therefore conceptualized as:

- Identifying a word with the same initial consonant sound as in a word given orally
- Identifying a word with the same final consonant sound as in a word given orally

- Identifying a word whose initial or final cluster or digraph has the same sound as in a word given orally
- Identifying a word with the same short or long medial vowel sound as in a given word

Even in today's "instruct/drill/test" educational climate, a great many kindergarten teachers, and some first and second grade teachers, provide for long periods of freely chosen activities such as pretend play; block building; language arts and math games; reading "real books" (as opposed to basal readers); painting; drawing; and writing labels, signs, journals, books, captions, sentence strips, and so forth. Teachers devoted to this philosophy of education ensure that reading, writing, spelling, math, and so on are threads that are woven through many activities initiated spontaneously by children.

A test item corresponding to the first objective is the word *door*, uttered and presented with four printed words: boy, day, tap, pork. The child is asked to choose the one word that begins with the same sound.

Even subtests called "Reading Comprehension" are in reality tests of decoding in the early grades. In a typical test item, the child is presented with the sentence "She is on the horse," followed by three pictures: a girl sitting on a horse, a girl standing by a horse, and a girl standing in front of a horse feeding it. The answer hinges on decoding the word *on*.

For modern psycholinguists, the objective in reading is the construction of meaning from print, in context. In the example given by Engel in Chapter 11, saying "It was a nice house" while trying to read "It was a nice *home*" is considered more sensible than saying, "It was a nice harm." However, both errors would be considered equally wrong in an achievement test. According to psycholinguistic theory (Smith, 1971), the sound a letter "makes" belongs to only one of the three systems the child uses in learning to read—the syntactic system, the semantic system, and the graphophonic system. The child who said "house" used the syntactic system to predict that "It was a nice" would be followed by a noun, the semantic system to predict that the noun would stand for something like a house, and the graphophonic system to think that *h*_____ must stand for "house." Makers of achievement tests are aware only of the graphophonic system and completely overlook the syntactic and semantic systems that children and adults use when they read.

Mathematics. Authors of textbooks and achievement tests think about mathematics as knowledge of mathematical symbols, rules, and conventions. Test makers therefore state objectives such as knowing the names of geometric shapes, the value of coins, time as shown by a clock, and the conventional units used to measure length, as we saw earlier. These are all examples of social knowledge that constitutes the most superficial aspects of mathematics. Leinwand gives other examples of test items in Chapter 8.

Paper-and-pencil tests cannot tap young children's logico-mathematical knowledge. While every achievement test yields a score on children's number concepts, these scores have almost nothing to do with number concepts. For example, one of the items to test children's number concepts is something like "Mark the one where the word says the same thing as the number: three-2, five-5, seven-3." This question taps children's ability to read (social knowledge) rather than their number concepts (logico-mathematical knowledge). The only way to

Table 2.1
Arithmetic Scores of Two Groups of Second Graders

	Traditional program N = 39	Constructivist program N = 46
Double-column addition		
Stanford Achievement Test		
Raw score on addition of whole		
numbers	15.12	14.76
Explanation of "carrying"		
("regrouping")	23%	83%
Misaligned digits	79%	11%
4		
35		
+24		
99		
Problem solving		
Stanford Achievement Test	12.76	12.62
1988 Math Sampler		
10 cars	29%	61%
294 labels	2%	20%
Estimation (4.5 seconds)		
347 + 282 (between 500 and 700)	39%	64%
Mental arithmetic (9 seconds)		
98 + 43	17%	48%

test children for number concepts is in interviews such as the one described earlier using beads and glasses.

Table 2.1 shows that different theories lead to different instructional goals, different methods of evaluation, and dramatically different conclusions about what children are learning. The table concerns two groups of second graders, one taught in the traditional way, and the other in the constructivist program described in Kamii (1985, 1989b).

In double-column addition, the two groups learned about the same amount according to the Stanford Achievement Test, by getting near-perfect raw scores of 15.12 and 14.76 respectively in addition of whole numbers. (The maximum possible score on this cluster is 16.)

When the children were asked in individual interviews to explain "carrying" ("regrouping"), however, 23% and 83% respectively were found to be able to explain their procedures. The interviewer gave each child a card on which "16 + 17" was written vertically and asked him to give the answer. After the child gave the answer of 33, two piles of 16 and 17 chips were presented, and the child was asked to explain his procedure. Three-fourths of the traditionally instructed children added 6 and 7 chips first, got a total of 13, "carried" one of the 13 chips instead of 10, and demonstrated $1 + 1 + 1$ instead of $10 + 10 + 10$. These children could easily get the correct answer of 33, but did not know the reason for the rules they were following. (The difference between the two groups, between 23% and 83%, was statistically significant at the .001 level of confidence.)

Each child then received a sheet on which the misaligned addition problem shown in Table 2.1 appeared. The interviewer asked the child to "read these numbers" and then to write the answer. When the child finished, the interviewer asked him or her to read the answer aloud and then inquired, "Does that sound right?" The proportions who wrote 99 for $(4 + 35 + 24)$ by mechanically following the rule of adding the columns were 79% for the traditionally instructed group and 11% for the constructivist group. (The difference was again statistically significant at the .001 level of confidence.)

We can see in the examples that if the goal is for the child to be able to get correct answers, the evaluator looks only for correct answers. If, on the other hand, the goal is for the child to think and to be able to justify her or his answer, the evaluator looks for evidence of ability to reason.

The Stanford Achievement Test has a cluster named Problem Solving. The mean raw scores in Problem Solving were 12.76 for the traditionally instructed group and 12.62 for the constructivist group (out of a maximum possible score of 15). These problems are all easy and familiar, as in the following typical example that we made up: Johnny bought 14 oranges and gave 5 of them to Suzie. How many does he have left?

When harder problems were asked in a group test that we made up and called the 1988 Math Sampler, the two groups again looked very different. Examples of harder questions are:

1. There are 49 children who want to go to the zoo. Some of their parents are willing to drive their cars and can take 5 children in each car. How many cars will be needed to take all 49 children to the zoo?
2. There are 21 children in the class. If they each bring 14 soup labels, how many labels will there be all together?

As can be seen in Table 2.1, the percentages of correct answers given were 29 and 61 respectively for the problem about the cars, and 2 and 20 respectively for the problem about soup labels. (The differences were statistically significant at the .002 and .004 levels respectively.)

Finally, the Stanford Achievement Test does not have a single question in estimation or mental arithmetic. When we gave 4.5 seconds to second graders to write an approximate answer for 347 + 282, 39% of the traditionally taught group and 64% of the constructivist group wrote answers between 500 and 700. (The difference between the two groups was statistically significant at the .01 level.) When the groups were given 9 seconds to do 98 + 43 mentally, 17% and 48%, respectively, wrote the correct answer. The difference (at the .002 level of significance) again demonstrates how different kinds of instructional objectives and test questions lead to dramatically different conclusions about what children are learning.

Social, moral, and attitudinal goals. Perhaps the most serious shortcoming of the use of achievement tests as accountability measures lies in the realm of social, moral, and attitudinal development. Clearly, schools have an impact on these dimensions of development, and too often an adverse impact. For example, the two groups of second graders discussed above were given the following question in the 1988 Math Sampler: "There are 26 sheep and 10 goats on a ship. How old is the captain?" One hundred percent of the traditionally taught children wrote "36" rather than writing that the question did not make sense. These children blindly manipulated the numbers instead of thinking critically about the question.

When a teacher walks around a classroom of first graders while they are filling out worksheets and stops to ask one of them how she or he got a particular answer, the child often reacts by grabbing an eraser and rubbing out the answer, even when it is perfectly correct. Already in first grade, many children have learned to distrust their own thinking, something far more basic than the so-called "basics."

The simplest test of children's social and moral autonomy is to ask the teacher to leave the classroom for 15 minutes. Autonomous children will go on with their activities, with or without the teacher's presence. Heteronomous children—those who have been trained to be controlled by others—soon explode in chaos. Achievement tests simply do not give any information about these kinds of differences in children's social, moral, and attitudinal development.

Achievement tests are not valid measures of accountability

The preceding discussion has given many reasons for our saying that achievement tests are not valid measures of accountability. In Chapter 1, Perrone also explains why the use of achievement tests cannot be defended for the evaluation of young children's learning. We would add that higher test scores can be obtained in at least two different ways — by fertilizing the entire field, to use an analogy with agriculture, and by fertilizing only soil samples.

Achievement tests are made so that half of the children at any grade level will, by definition, come out below the average. The children who come out below the average are those who are developing more slowly than the others for a variety of reasons. It is widely known that children develop at different rates, whether the skill acquisition being looked at is walking, talking, reading, or learning mathematical concepts.

The first kind of higher test scores is the result of good instruction and/or a desirable home environment. For example, many teachers and parents who have never heard of contructivism stimulate children's interest in books and written words and encourage them to write with "invented" spelling. As a result of this encouragement, many first graders get to the level of being able to select the correct answer out of "nit," "nite," "night," and "nyte."

The second way of getting higher test scores, fertilizing only soil samples, is unfortunately what is happening in most schools today. Many teachers drill children on the words that are on the spelling test. Teaching the test or to the test is like fertilizing only soil samples instead of the entire field. It is truly tragic that even after the publication of *Nationally Normed Elementary Achievement Testing in America's Public Schools: How All Fifty States Are Above the National Average* (Cannell, 1987), most people still think that rising test scores is good news.

Achievement testing results in practices that are harmful to children's development

To evaluate a child's intellectual progress, we should compare his or her knowledge at one point in time with the knowledge at another point in time. The interval between the two points may be one year, six months, or six weeks. However, the use of achievement tests involves the comparison of children at only one point in time. Whether scores are reported in stanines, percentiles, or grade levels (see Chapter 1), these numbers are all derived from comparisons of numbers of correct answers given by children of the same grade level at one point in time.

Achievement tests are made so that half of the children at any grade level will, by definition, come out below the average. The children who come out below the average are those who are developing more slowly than the others for a variety of reasons. It is widely known that children develop at different rates, whether the acquisition be walking, talking, reading, or learning sums.

Because achievement tests are designed to make half of the children come out below the average, they include many questions that only small percentages of children answer correctly. When the pressure is on to raise test scores, teachers have to get children to give correct answers to more difficult questions at increasingly earlier ages. To push chil-

Figure 2.1
The Relationships Between Behaviorism and Constructivism and Between the Geocentric and Heliocentric Theories

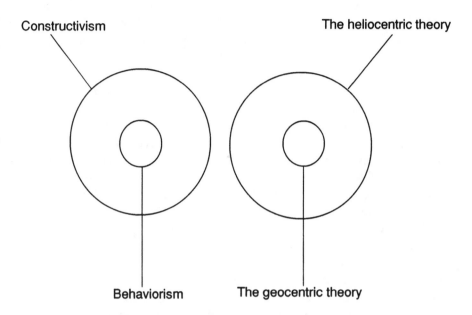

Constructivism   The heliocentric theory

Behaviorism   The geocentric theory

dren to give correct answers, teachers usually use drills, which are based on behaviorism and associationism.

Behaviorism and constructivism

Behaviorism is a scientific theory of learning that states in essence that animals, including human beings, learn through repetition and the effective use of reward and/or punishment. Many versions of behaviorism exist, but they are similar in that they attempt to specify the conditions under which animals change specific behaviors. Associationism is similar to behaviorism but is less systematic.

Figure 2.1 schematically illustrates the relationship between behaviorism and constructivism. This figure shows that constructivism can explain everything behaviorism can, but that the converse is not true. For example, constructivism can explain animals' learning through reward and punishment by pointing out that all animals adapt to their environment. However, behaviorism cannot explain children's construction of number concepts or their learning to say "Markie me pushed" or to write "GYNS" for *genius*. Likewise, behaviorism can explain heteronomy, but not the autonomy of a Martin Luther King. Only constructivism can explain why King acted on his convictions in spite of the police, jails, dogs, water hoses, and threats of assassination.

Much of the content in early childhood education can be taught either with behavioristic principles or with constructivist principles. For example, teachers can drill children to memorize letter names, initial consonants, final consonants, initial digraphs, short vowels, long vowels, sums, rules for double-column addition, and so on. However, teachers can also encourage children to make their own connections among words that are of interest *to them*. For example, Benny was excited to find out at Easter time that *Bunny* was written like *Benny*. He also told his teacher that Nora Benson's last name was similar to his first name *and* his last name, Garson. Constructivist teachers encourage children to use what they already know to figure out what they want to write. In arithmetic likewise, constructivist teachers do not teach rules for double-column addition; instead, they encourage children to use their knowledge of $10 + 10$ to figure out how to do $10 + 12$.

Achievement testing encourages teachers to use behavioristic principles even more heavily than before. The result, as we saw in Table 2.1, is children who can give correct answers but cannot explain why their answer is correct. When presented with misaligned digits, the great majority who had been drilled to follow rules blindly followed the prescribed behavioral sequence.

The relationship between behaviorism and constructivism is analogous to the one between the geocentric theory (that the planets and the sun revolve around the Earth) and the heliocentric theory (that the Earth and the planets revolve around the sun). As shown in Figure 2.1, the heliocentric theory went beyond the geocentric theory by encompassing it rather than by replacing it. This is why we still hear of sunset and sunrise in the weather forecast. Within the limited perspective of Earth, it is still true that the sun sets and rises. Likewise, within the limited perspective of observable, surface behavior, it is still true that children can be taught by repetition, reward, and/or punishment.

Behaviorism is rooted in common sense, just as the geocentric theory is rooted in common sense. According to traditional common sense, children acquire knowledge and moral values directly from the environment, one by one in ready-made forms. On the basis of this traditional assumption, behaviorists and test makers define goals and objectives in a juxtaposed, fragmented way. Just as navigation worked for many centuries within the geocentric framework, education has "worked" for centuries within the framework of common sense and behaviorism. The time has come, however, to look below the surface of "correct" behaviors. Educators must conceptualize their goals in terms of children's deep sense of self in relation to others, and the depths and breadth of their beliefs and understandings.

Educators must conceptualize their goals in terms of children's deep sense of self in relation to others, and the depth and breadth of their beliefs and understandings.

In conclusion

Many people say that achievement testing can stop only when better instruments are offered to replace achievement tests. We do not agree with this statement because using a better instrument would be like putting a better cart in front of the horse. As long as educators feel compelled to make themselves look good in short-term evaluations, they will go on with behaviorism and associationism, which produce quick results.

The authors of this book are calling for a halt to achievement testing because we as educators must first reconceptualize our goals and reexamine our principles of teaching. The questions we need to answer *clearly* before looking for new instruments to measure accountability are: Do we want autonomous or heteronomous adults? How does autonomy develop? Do moral and intellectual development happen separately in the classroom? Can we drill children and turn out critical, independent, creative, and honest thinkers? And do drilling and memorization have anything to do with children's sense of self, the drug problem, teen-age pregnancies, and the drop-out problem?

Chapter 3

The Dilemma for Superintendents

Eugene W. Thompson

I t is not easy for the superintendent to counter a board decision that says the way to improve the quality of elementary schools is to begin testing as soon as those 4- and 5-year-old students arrive in September. It is especially difficult if the superintendent does not fully understand why such testing is not a good idea. Most of the time, it may be easier to sidestep this type of tough, volatile issue than to stand against such a politically popular position.

Superintendents' lack of child development training contributes to the problem

The superintendent needs to understand the nature of children, learning, and testing. These difficult, ambiguous pieces of knowledge are essential for anyone who is to provide leadership on an issue such as early childhood testing. Yet, these are the very issues on which many superintendents, lacking the background, feel insecure. Few states mandate extensive child development training for superintendent certification. Ohio, for example, has one of the most closely defined programs for superintendent certification training in the nation; yet it mandates only the one standard course in human growth and development, while requiring at least a half-dozen courses in various aspects of law and finance. Similarly, evaluation training is generally limited to one course in research design/statistics with virtually no coverage of test construction or capability. The recent report of the National Policy Board for Educational Administration (1989) entitled *Improving the Preparation of School Administrators: An Agenda for Reform* points out the obvious need to focus administrator training on "the core function of

the school: teaching and learning" (p. 20). The superintendent's inse-
curities and inadequacies in the area of early childhood education,
coupled with a politically unstable environment, often prevent the
superintendent from providing the leadership necessary to ensure the
best educational environment for children.

Superintendents' traditional career track contributes to the problem

Working with small children in early childhood and elementary
education is often viewed as a role for women; men who choose this
aspect of education are frequently seen as less assertive or less traditionally masculine. The typical superintendent comes from the secondary school ranks, often with little knowledge of early childhood education. The generally more assertive or aggressive style of high school
administrators enables them to compete more successfully for a superintendency. More superintendents are emerging from elementary positions, but the shift is slight and it will take decades before it has a
significant impact on education.

In essence, career track and lack of understanding of the early testing
issue combine to encourage the superintendent to step to the side. In
the interest of good politics on the bigger issues, it becomes easier to
allow politicians to deliver emotional rhetoric that results in programs
harmful to young children.

Personal conviction and political skill are critical in confronting the testing games grown-ups play

It takes courage, the ability to persuade, political savvy, and, most
important, personal conviction to oppose a politically popular position.
The superintendent needs to clearly understand the issues involved
with norm-referenced achievement testing in early childhood, and how
such tests are constructed, what impact basic measurement concepts
have on test data, and the nature of learning in early childhood. In
order to counter the demand for young child testing, the superintendent needs well-thought-out alternatives that will demonstrate the
effectiveness of the education dollar.

It takes courage, the ability to persuade, political savvy, and, most important, personal conviction to oppose a politically popular position. The superintendent needs to clearly understand the issues involved with norm-referenced achievement testing in early childhood, how such tests are constructed, what impact basic measurement concepts have on test data, and the nature of learning in early childhood.

In short, the superintendent must be a political animal. Counting support votes is an incessant activity. I have always said that, when working with a seven-member board, I listen politely to one member, closely to two, intently to three, and take action when four agree. The superintendent's survival as a leader depends a great deal upon the political skills of persuasion and leadership. The superintendent must be a skilled performer in what may be a threatening environment.

Board members like to see scores. Members are usually lay people with little understanding of how learning occurs, much less of testing and measurement. They often assume that if scores are going up, learning must be taking place; higher test scores often become their goal. The superintendent must use precise political skills mixed with cool courage to maneuver through this minefield of assumptions.

Why do top level school executives permit the use of norm-referenced tests to determine educational programs for young children? To answer this question, one must understand the nature of public school superintendency as it exists today.

Boards hire superintendents. The members who hire a superintendent tend to be committed to the success of that superintendent. However, there seems to be an increasing tendency among board members to serve only one or at the most two terms. Since as many as three seats may become available on a seven-member board at an annual election, the superintendent can quickly be without the strong supporters who took part in the hiring process. The board may then feel no personal commitment to the superintendent and no need to defend him or her on emotional issues such as testing. They may take the popular position that schools must do a better job, and that the only way to ensure their accountability is to measure the product as is done in the private sector. After all, they say, look what Lee Iaccoca did for quality at Chrysler! You just need to measure your product—young children—and make sure that the teachers work harder!

Because of the stress associated with the superintendent's tenure, public school superintendency can be a fertile ground for paranoia. It tends to be a lonely, pressure-filled role. The superintendent's office is an arena in which paranoia can grow into almost paralyzing anxiety. I have felt it. I have seen it in colleagues.

The truth is the threat may be real. There are disgruntled labor groups, athletic boosters upset over losing seasons, parents distressed at reductions in transportation services, merchants and residents convinced that taxes are too high, and the many concerns of other constituent groups served by a school district, to say nothing of the internal assassins. I have been a superintendent of a small rural district and an urban deputy superintendent, and many decisions I made cost me support. In five years a support base can be seriously eroded. Still, a responsible educational leader has no choice but to take a stand. Trying to walk down the middle of the road simply increases the likelihood of being hit by traffic from both directions.

Dealing effectively with the media is not easy, but is a must

Within the intense political arena, the superintendent must contend with the loudest voice of all—the media. A savvy superintendent counseled me once, "Don't fight with people who buy ink by the barrel." The superintendent must, in fact, work with the media. Personally, my experience has been good. I have never been misquoted, and I have never been quoted when I asked to be "off the record." I have, however, been lambasted by anonymous employees and board members quoted by reporters. By and large, the press has treated me fairly. Still, it seems that many of the problems we are facing relative to the testing frenzy in early childhood stem from the media presentation.

Reports of declining test scores help to sell newspapers. These reports make for catchy headlines and feed into the post-Watergate pillorying of public officials. If superintendents have a problem understanding norm-referenced tests, reporters and editors grasp even less. Part of the superintendent's job in working with the media is to educate the reporter assigned to the schools. If you do not do this job well, you have one large problem on hand.

Interestingly, I have found that the most fervent consumer of the test report is the real estate agent. Many agents want to identify the area with the "best" school, based upon test data. While reporters generally make an attempt at understanding the test report, real estate agents are rarely bothered by such fine detail. Their goal seems to be to rank the schools as quickly as possible. With the school district test report in hand, they feel they can prove to their clients that the home for sale is in the area with the "best" school.

Juggling the need for accountability, inappropriate tests, dollars, and all sorts of pressures

Norm-referenced testing of young children is inappropriate. The use of such measures to assess individual student learning at any level, move children to the next level, or determine teacher effectiveness is pure folly. What is needed is a wider based evaluation process. Development of such a process is expensive. This predicament is a familiar one! Dollars must be found. Few superintendents propose annual budgets with more than 0.1% devoted to evaluation. In the private sector, a figure of 10% for evaluation is more common. The dollar commitment to the development of evaluation techniques that are more broadly based than the easy-to-administer and relatively inexpensive norm-referenced tests is essential. Because they are not labor intensive, requiring only one evaluator for perhaps 25 students, these tests require a far lower per-pupil expenditure than more extensive evaluation procedures.

We do need to evaluate. We do need to be accountable. In a time when an annual per-pupil expenditure of $5,000 in major urban areas is not rare, we do need to provide a measure through which success, or lack thereof, is determined. The superintendent has the responsibility of providing public assessments of the schools. The problem is how to do this.

We need to move away from norm-referenced testing of young children entirely, and sharply reduce the use of norm-referenced tests *generally,* while increasing evaluation efforts throughout public education. Means of assessing

- children's attitudes and self-esteem,
- school climate,
- teacher expectations, and
- parent involvement

are available and can be used for evaluation purposes. *We know these to be the critical facets of the learning environment, yet we do little to determine the degree to which they are present in a positive manner.* Research about effective schools has been available for years, yet little has been done to assist our schools in meeting these criteria. We have made virtually no effort to evaluate the school climate created by the building administrator although this variable has been identified as the critical factor in student learning. The superintendent's task is to know what teachers' expectations of their students are, to know how parents feel about the schools, and to know the degree to which child learning meets district curriculum, *and then to communicate the information openly and honestly to politicians, reporters, real estate agents, parents, and board members.*

We need to move away from norm-referenced testing of young children entirely, and sharply reduce the use of norm-referenced tests generally, while increasing evaluation efforts throughout public education. Means of assessing children's attitudes and self-esteem, school climate, teacher expectations, and parent involvement are available and can be used for evaluation purposes. We know these to be the critical facets of the learning environment, yet we do little to determine the degree to which they are present in a positive manner. *Superintendents need to lead.*

Superintendents need to lead

Proposals to expand the evaluation process of schools must come from the superintendent's office. The uses of norm-referenced achievement tests to determine whether or not a young child will be advanced a grade or grouped with the bluebirds or buzzards can be curtailed only with sound proposals from an astute political leader. When decisions are made regarding young children, they must be made using the best available information. Political leaders of education need to ensure that young children are not made victims of a testing system.

Superintendents must do what they are hired to do: They must lead. They must lead the educational community to an understanding of the inability of norm-referenced tests to provide usable data regarding young children.

1. The superintendent must provide board members with professional publications that discuss in lay terms the dangers of attempting to define young children's needs using simplistic tests and set up training sessions to meet the same goal.
2. The superintendent must see to it that staff development sessions prepared cooperatively with local universities are presented for district personnel. Teachers and principals must be provided with the opportunity to develop understandings of the fallacies in determining the children's futures by testing.
3. The superintendent must provide leadership to ensure that parent training sessions are prepared to enable parents to develop like understandings. We have too often convinced parents that their own observations of their children's learning are secondary to the "hard" data supplied by norm-referenced tests. These beliefs must be reversed through community training.
4. The superintendent must ensure that the media and other influential people in the community are educated through press conferences and invitations to attend training opportunities.

The task of educating the community is large. The potential benefits for young children are worth the effort and energies of those who hold the leadership roles in our school districts.

The political structure is in place. State level superintendent organizations routinely maintain professional lobbyists and routinely organize breakfasts and luncheons with key political leaders. It is a woeful county educational office that cannot activate a telephone call system involving every local superintendent within the service area. Local superintendents regularly receive the notice to make a call to the local political representative urging a vote in the state house on an educational issue. Superintendents simply must activate the system for the good of young children as well as on finance or legal issues.

The task of altering beliefs and changing long-held convictions is not easy. As a society we have often sought the quick and easy solution to complex problems. Our schools reflect our society. Tests and test scores have long been perceived as the measure of success of our schooling process. For over a generation Scholastic Aptitude Test scores have been the standard by which our secondary schools were measured. The transition to the use of such tests with young children was seemingly natural and probably predictable. The assumptions that led to this transition were false. Norm-referenced tests are neither valid nor reliable within acceptable limits when used with children 7, 6, 5 years old and even younger. It is the responsibility of superintendents as community educational leaders to communicate this message.

Superintendents choose their leadership roles. The role is known to be one of high risk and intense stress. These role characteristics do not excuse the superintendent from the responsibility to lead on sensitive issues. Morally, the superintendent is obligated to lead. Ethically, such leadership can be neither avoided nor declined. When the superintendent accepts his or her position, he or she also accepts the responsibility to speak on behalf of young children. This responsibility requires the superintendent to speak against the potential damage to children caused by the misuse of norm-referenced tests.

Chapter 4

The Approach of a School System

Shirley P. Grover

For a leader of an organization to be effective, there must be a good fit between the beliefs, values, and aspirations of the members and those of the leader. In the case of a superintendent of schools, the need for a good fit means that the superintendent's world view has to match in some way the community's belief systems, values, and aspirations. This first comes into play when a superintendent interviews for the position. The superintendent has to know her or his own values and beliefs and make sure that there are some shared views and common beliefs about what education is and what the school system should be doing. The closer the fit, the more likely the superintendent will be successful in carrying out what she or he wants to do in a school system. For example, a person who does not believe in the testing game so many educators are playing today would not strive to be hired as superintendent in a district that focused only on test scores.

When I went to the Scarborough School Department, I looked for a school board that believed the same things I did about the purposes and aims of education, how teachers ought to be treated, and how change ought to take place. I made sure that the school board wanted children to learn more than just basic skills. Evidence of a good match between Scarborough and me existed not only in what the school board said to me but also in the written statement of the school system's philosophy. The philosophy statement implied that the board believed children should be treated as individuals and that children should become autonomous, problem-solving adults. The school board and I thus seemed to be headed in the same direction.

The superintendent also has to understand the bigger picture of the community. For example, she or he has to know whether the school board really represents the community and has to understand the dynamics of the community as a whole. When I arrived, Scarborough's socioeconomic patterns were in flux. The community had long been the home of fishermen, farmers, and blue collar workers. Many people with seemingly higher income and education were now moving into town. They typically had different demands for their children's education.

Once a good match is found and a superintendent enters a school system, it is important not to mandate change. Rather than dictating that things be different, an effective superintendent looks for an opening where he or she can introduce the kind of change that people will support. That opening can come from parents or teachers. In Scarborough, when parents came to us and talked about wanting something different for young children, we saw an opening. At that time, there was a movement to create prekindergarten classes for children considered "not mature enough" for kindergarten. There was also a movement to create transitional first and second grade classes for children who would otherwise have to repeat a grade. When parents in Scarborough asked for a prekindergarten and transitional first and second grade classes, it was the time to talk with them and teachers about different ways of arranging for learning experiences for young children. It was an opportunity for us to talk about how children really learn and what kinds of activities are good for their development. This was our way of introducing constructivist ideas without using technical terms.

A superintendent has to keep in touch with the forces at the national and state levels, too. The movement at the national level was for choices among public schools, with vouchers and tuition tax credit. I took the notion of choice and said we should have choices within our public schools: We should continue to offer a traditional program to parents, teachers, and children who wanted it and should also introduce the idea of a constructivist program for those who wanted something different.

Some parents who were economically more advantaged were already exercising other choices for their children's education by sending them to private schools. Private schools do not necessarily have constructivist philosophies, but some have constructivist-like activities for children, with more hands-on, activity-based, relevant learning, and more group efforts, or cooperative learning. I proposed to the school board that we offer a choice within the school system between a multiage, constructivist program and a traditional one for children 5 to 7 years of age (corresponding to grades K–2). The board readily accepted and supported this idea. In fact, the board could easily see how the constructivist classroom would appeal to some parents, who would view it as a better opportunity for their young children.

As superintendent, I proposed to the school board that we offer a choice within the school system between a multiage, constructivist program and a traditional one for children 5 to 7 years of age (corresponding to grades K–2). The board readily accepted and supported this idea. In fact, the board could easily see how the constructivist classroom would appeal to some parents, who would view it as a better opportunity for their young children.

Introducing a multiage, constructivist program

First, we went to teachers and principals and talked about how children learn and develop and how we wanted to develop a new framework of putting 5-, 6-, and 7-year-olds together. Scarborough has three small primary schools, and we chose the one that was centrally located so that we could bus perhaps 80 children to it during the first year. We thought 80 would be a good number initially because we believed parents of only about 80 children would choose the new program, out of the 450 primary age children we were expecting in the fall of 1986. We planned to add a new group of kindergartners to the new program in 1987 and 1988.

After describing our ideas, the Curriculum Director and I told the teachers that we would like some volunteers to work with us in developing the new program and fleshing out the framework. Ten teachers volunteered, so we devised an instrument to select those who had the greatest chance of success — those who were more flexible, and who seemed to be more frustrated with textbooks, workbooks, and pre-primers. We thus selected six teachers for the first year.

Then we held three evening meetings, one in each of the three schools, and asked parents to come. The Curriculum Director, some teachers, a few board members, and I presented the idea of a choice between a traditional program and a constructivist school, which we called G.O.L.D. for "Grouping for Optimal Learning Development." We explained that in the G.O.L.D. program we would assemble children in a multiage, nongraded setting and give more hands-on, activity-based, relevant-learning opportunities. We told them we would not use textbooks and would try not to use worksheets, and that the children would stay with the same teacher for three years. With that general description, we asked parents to sign up for the new program if they wanted to do so. We made it clear that the choice was entirely theirs.

Instead of 80 children, we got over 200 signed up for the G.O.L.D. program. I then decided that we should try to talk parents out of it. The school board and I felt that the parents were not necessarily choosing the program. Some were placing their children in the program because of the location of the school, others because their neighbors' children were going, and others because it was the "innovative" thing to do. But the more I tried to talk them out of the program, the more they wanted it; so we decided to have the G.O.L.D. program in the centrally located school as originally planned as well as in half of another school. We went back to the teachers and asked for more volunteers for the G.O.L.D. program.

Staff development

When teachers cannot depend on textbook series and workbooks to know what to do, teaching is much more difficult. An essential part of a constructivist program is teachers who understand children's learning and development and who can make decisions depending on the children's interests, personalities, and levels of cognitive development. In-service teacher education is, therefore, a critical part of initiating a constructivist program.

Staff development for the G.O.L.D. program began in the spring of 1986. The Curriculum Director and I wrote a proposal and submitted it to the State. We had monies from the school board to begin the program and carry it out, but we needed some outside monies to provide a concrete vision and an incentive for teachers—something special that would keep them going when the going got tough. Typically in the change process, there are times when things get harder and people get down. The grant from the State was to send teachers to England to observe some British infant schools for two weeks. British infant schools are for children equivalent in age to children in kindergarten, first, and second grade in the United States. The educational philosophy on which they operate is akin to the American Progressive Education movement earlier in the 20th Century, and to constructivism.

We wanted to send teachers to England before the new program started in September 1986, but there were problems in England at that time and we decided to go the following summer. This change in plans turned out to be fortunate because it gave the teachers a chance to experience the new program for a year, to formulate new questions for themselves, and to know what to seek. Meanwhile, the G.O.L.D. program added new teachers in the summer of 1987 because of a new group of 5-year-olds; half of the kindergarten population chose the program. Some of the new teachers came from private schools. When they heard about our nongraded, multiage program, they applied to work in it. We were delighted to have these teachers and took them to England, too.

The staff development activities were led sometimes by teachers with special knowledge and skills, and sometimes by the Curriculum Director, who supported the teachers on a day-to-day basis, asking questions to keep them going in the right direction and helping them when they physically rearranged their classrooms. We also used consultants from outside, who are very important. On the one hand, there are plenty of consultants selling packages and ready-made programs, but those salespeople do not help teachers better understand how children develop. On the other hand are theoreticians; teachers need theory, but people who know theory can often not translate it into classroom practice. A superintendent cannot be disheartened if theorists who know practice are hard to get. They must be found and brought to the school system. Consultation must continue over a period of time rather than being one-shot deals.

The staff development activities were led sometimes by teachers with special knowledge and skills, and sometimes by the Curriculum Director, who supported the teachers on a day-to-day basis, asking questions to keep them going in the right direction and helping them when they physically rearranged their classrooms. We also used consultants from outside, who are very important.

Although consultants and people within the school system bring new knowledge and new ways of thinking, they do not tell teachers what to do. Teachers have to make decisions about classroom practice. For example, when some teachers asked me if they had to have recess, I said, "I don't know. Do you have to have recess?" They said that the traditional school had to have recess, whereupon I asked, "Who said so?" Their reply was "The office." I told them that the office now said they did not have to have recess if they did not want it. I went on to ask, "Why do you think recess got there to begin with?" and the teachers talked about children needing to release energy after sitting for a long time. I asked the teachers if their children would be sitting for long periods of time, and they replied, "Of course not." So I asked if they thought recess would be necessary. They thought not, but when fall came, they had recess. When they are unsure, teachers fall back on what they know. Even if there is no real reason for recess, they still continue to do what they have always known. When recess came, however, the children did not want to stop doing what they were doing; so the teachers learned that recess was not necessary and decided to either abandon it or at least allow the children to choose. Neither children nor adults learn to be autonomous by being told what to do or what to say.

Kurt Lewin said that behavior is a function of the person in the environment. In-service teacher education can change the person, or a teacher's beliefs and knowledge, but the person's behavior, or teaching, will not change much unless the environment in which a teacher works is changed. The environment includes the physical setting, such as the arrangement of desks and chairs, and resources, such as textbooks and workbooks. The environment also includes the kinds of children put in a classroom, and it makes a difference whether there are only 5-year-olds in a room or a range of 5-, 6-, and 7-year-olds. If administrators want to change teachers' behavior, they have to change the environment in which teachers work. It is not enough just to provide in-service teacher education.

Just as teachers set up the environment for children to facilitate their learning, we try to set up the environment to maximize teachers' growth. When we send teachers to conferences, we send them in pairs so that they will have a chance to exchange viewpoints. We also encourage them to make presentations about the G.O.L.D. program because by sharing ideas they clarify their own thinking and strengthen their knowing. We continue to work at developing our program by visiting other places and by identifying appropriate practices. Having participated in the Prospect School program in Vermont, we now want to set up the kind of child-study teams that we saw there. A child-study team is a group of teachers who get together to study individual children in depth and to exchange ideas about educational plans. The exchanges of viewpoints in case studies contribute enormously to the growth of teachers, who are otherwise isolated from each other in separaate classrooms. We also wish to increase the use of videotaping and the amount of time teachers have to think and talk with each other during the day. Collaboration is vital to teachers' growth.

Staff reactions

Teachers must feel support for what they do and superintendents must extend that support. As an advocate of choice within our public schools, I also have to make sure I support both programs. My expressed preference for a particular program could easily be mistaken as nonsupport for the other. Teachers do, for example, count the number of laudatory adjectives used to describe our new program and find fewer such adjectives used in describing the traditional one. I tell parents and teachers that if they think one program is better for them, that *is* the program that is right for them. This is tied to my belief that we each have our developmental stages that we move through at different times. Some teachers are comfortable in their current stage of development, and if that is the graded school, I support them in that. I do not support failure to grow and develop *further*, but I support each teacher where she is and try to give her what she needs to do what she believes it best to do. I try to encourage teachers to get into new things. For example, all teachers are invited to the G.O.L.D. staff development activities. My hope is that by participating in the G.O.L.D. training or other like activities, teachers will reflect on what they are doing and feel the need to do something different.

Parents' reactions

When half of the parents choose a new program, this is evidence that there is a need for it and that they value that kind of education. Many parents first accepted the program without knowing what it would actually entail. But teachers needed parents in the classroom to help during the first year, and parents saw what it was really like. These parents sold the program to other parents. When children sing as they go home at the end of the day, parents do not have to ask what kind of day their child had.

We organized a parents' advisory group, which is a very important group. Like teachers, parents, too, need each other for support. A parent would often say, "I knew how my child was doing in the traditional school because I could decorate my refrigerator with worksheets and all the papers that said 'Good' or had stars on them. The traditional school also gave report cards. But now I don't necessarily know what my child is doing in school." However, another parent would say that a parent knows when a child can make connections between what happens in school and what happens in life. For example, one child had tried to read labels on packages and asked if that was what the writing said. Another mother who had an older child in the same school said that the older child never made such connections or showed initiative by volunteering that $1 + 1 = 2$, $2 + 2 = 4$, $4 + 4 = 8$, and so on.

We do not give report cards with grades on them. Instead, our report cards give information about where children are in mathematics and literacy development, how well they work alone and in small and large groups, where they are in Piagetian cognitive development, and so forth. Parents now have more information than they ever had, but they sometimes still ask how their child compares to the other children. We try hard not to compare one child with the others. We want children to develop naturally at their own rate, so we say, "This is how much progress your child has made." The report card has gone through two or three revisions to date.

A lesson

One of the teachers was interested in gardening as part of a theme. He wrote a proposal for a grant and got some tools, and the children talked about what it meant to plant and grow vegetables and where they would house their tools. When they discovered that the school did not have a space to store equipment, the teacher invited a man who built houses with no nails to speak to the class. The man showed them a model of a little barn where they could put their tools, and the 5-, 6-, and 7-year-olds asked him if he would come and build a little barn outside. The man volunteered and brought his three assistants and equipment and donated the wood to build the barn.

But first the children had to go to the school board to ask for permission to build the structure on school grounds and to the town hall to get a permit. They decided to elect their own spokesperson and went to an official school board meeting that was shown on cable television. The teacher did not speak; the children went to the microphone to explain why they wanted their little barn. The school board listened, questioned the children, and voted to allow them to build their structure. The next week, the children went to the town hall and asked for a permit. The confidence of those 5-, 6-, and 7-year-olds taking ownership, feeling independent and competent, and working together was unbelievable.

Some parents who were economically more advantaged were already exercising other choices for their children's education by sending them to private schools. Private schools do not necessarily have constructivist philosophies, but some have constructivist-like activities for children, with more hands-on, activity-based, relevant learning, and more group efforts, in cooperative learning.

Evaluation

We give a standardized achievement test at the second grade but don't put much weight on the scores. We recognize that these tests are but one simple measure taken at one instance that can, by no means, reflect all that a child truly knows. The test is given mainly to assure people that the children in the nongraded program do not score any less well than those in the graded school.

Ever since the program started, we believed that we should broaden and vary our assessments. From the beginning, teachers and parents remarked that the children in the G.O.L.D. program were generally happier, more curious, and more confident. We designed instruments for teachers to interview children and for parents to interview their children. We also gave a self-concept instrument to children in both programs. We now have a grant to assess children's development in math and in literacy, in the kinds of thinking they do, their ability to cooperate with other people, their sense of self, their feeling of competence, and so on. The data from the third year are now being analyzed with the help of the University of Southern Maine. These data are on the first group of children, who have been in the G.O.L.D. program for three years.

In conclusion

It is truly easier for educators to continue doing what they have always done. The current reform movement in the early grades is not calling for more of the same thing (Bredekamp, 1987; NAEYC, 1988a; National Association of State Boards of Education, 1988). Progress requires that we change the way we think about children and their learning and development. If we really want to improve education, we cannot think in terms of more of the same things, quick fixes, or models to imitate. Teachers often say, "Show us how to do it. Show us a school that we can emulate," and I say, "That school is within you. Trust and do what you know is right for the children. Work at it, continually examine it, and you will make it better every year." It takes time to construct a constructivist school. In reality you never complete one, but you can get closer and closer with the help and support of other people who also believe in developing the potential that children bring to school.

Chapter 5

The Dilemma for Principals

Dode Morgan-Worsham

ecisions related to testing are almost always made by someone other than the school principal. In most cases the principal is in the position of simply having to follow the mandates of the district and to implement a testing program about which he or she has had little or no input. Which tests to administer, when, and to whom are decisions made by a state department, school board, superintendent of schools, and/or a central office department of testing.

This chapter examines some issues surrounding achievement testing of young children from the perspective of elementary school principals. In addition to sharing my own views as an elementary school principal, I will present the results of a survey given to other principals related to the same issues.

Data from tests are now used to measure the educational successes of states, districts, schools, principals, teachers, and students. Decisions regarding curriculum, program funding, salaries, and even whether or not a student is passed from one grade level to the next are often based on test scores. In an official newsletter of the Association for Supervision and Curriculum Development, its Executive Director, Gordon Cawelti (1988), stated, "One need only examine news accounts on testing each week to realize that standard testing practices are out of control and must be revamped" (p. 2). Following is an account of achievement testing that went out of control publicly in my own school district of Clark County, in which Las Vegas is located.

Winning at the testing game — Las Vegas style

In the spring of 1986 questions arose because achievement test scores in some schools appeared to be too high compared to students' ability scores. In other words, there was a large discrepancy between how students could be expected to perform based on their ability scores and how they actually performed on the achievement tests. The media gained knowledge of these discrepancies, and accusations of cheating spread across television and newspaper headlines.

Principals felt a new kind of pressure. Instead of worrying that test scores might be too low, the new concern was that they might be too high. Clark County ended up with the unique distinction in the country of feeling the pressure for lower test scores.

As a result of the controversy, the school board and central office administration called for a full examination of all testing practices throughout the school district. A committee made up of parents, community leaders, teachers, and administrators examined this critical issue. The committee dealt with such concerns as how test data were being used, the effects of testing on classroom practices, and the feelings of pressure on the part of principals, teachers, and students regarding test scores.

The process of reviewing and examining testing practices was time consuming and costly, but the results were positive. Changes that occurred included an affirmation from the school board and higher level administration that test scores would not be used to evaluate schools or teachers but instead would be used as a benchmark to compare our district with other districts across the nation. Whether the pressure to produce higher test scores was ever real or only imagined, this explicit statement seemed to alleviate principals' anxiety about test scores.

Feelings of pressure were further reduced as a result of other changes such as not reporting scores by individual classes and changing the time of testing from the spring to the fall so that teachers would not feel compelled to get children ready for tests through most of the year. However, as long as scores are publicly reported by the media, administrators and teachers still feel pressure, not necessarily from central office administration, but from the community and parents.

Although some positive changes have been made in Clark County, I believe that the major issues surrounding testing have yet to be addressed. These include whether or not standardized tests are the best means to assess student learning, especially 5- to 7-year-old children's

The process of reviewing and examining testing practices is costly and time consuming, but coupled with extensive education of teachers, parents, and the public, it can result in developmentally appropriate education for young children. Knowing this, each principal can lead the effort to question excessive testing in her or his school and look for viable alternatives.

learning, and how tests affect classroom practices. These are critical issues that need to be addressed at a national level. Since the first of these questions is discussed in Chapter 2, I will focus below on the second problem from the perspective of a principal.

The impact of testing on classroom practices

The real or perceived pressure to produce high test scores has a significant impact on instructional practices. In many classrooms an inordinate amount of time is spent in getting "ready for the test." Teachers prepare worksheets to provide 5-, 6-, and 7-year-olds with format practice and drill children on memorized rules and facts. Children need to know these rules and facts not because they fit the curriculum or are good for children, but because they are on the test.

While visiting a first grade classroom one morning, I observed a lesson on missing addends, such as $4 + \underline{\hspace{1cm}} = 7$. Children were struggling with what they were being asked to do and the teacher was visibly frustrated. Afterward, when I discussed the lesson with the teacher, I was faced with the reality of how testing indeed affects classroom practice. I asked the teacher why she thought the children were having such a difficult time with missing addends. She replied without hesitation, "Most first graders can't do missing addends, but it's on the test; so I must teach it before April."

As a result of the emphasis on test scores, instructional decisions are being made that do not support what is known about how children learn. Teachers and administrators must decide whether to implement instructional programs based on sound learning theory that may not produce high test scores, or to succumb to the pressures of testing and use programs that are known to raise test scores.

Ohanian (1984) says, "It is impossible to gauge the insidious effect testing has on the regular curriculum. Even the best teacher feels pressured to expose children to things test writers deem important" (p. 41). When a great deal of time is spent on drilling children on facts, giving timed tests, and adjusting curriculum content for the sake of the test, children's education suffers. Instruction that fosters thinking, understanding, and meaning is lost because teachers decide that there just isn't time for everything. Providing opportunities within the classroom for children to construct their own knowledge takes far more time than activities that center on rote drill and memorization.

The teaching of test-taking techniques, such as "If you don't know, just guess," or "When in doubt, mark (b)," communicates to students that scores are more important than knowledge. The same is true when teachers use commercial test-preparation materials. The message of the primacy of "right" answers is clear both to children and to teachers.

The school principal is in a pivotal position to take a stand in support of sound instructional decisions and therefore must stop participating in the pass-the-buck testing game. Instructional decisions must reflect what is best for children, not the push to raise test scores. Taking such a stand is not easy, however. It is hard to defend a position against standardized tests to supervisors, parents, and the community when local newspapers publish test scores as evidence of educational success. Taking such a position tends to be viewed as a "cop out" to defend lower test scores.

Findings from a survey

In the spring of 1988, in an attempt to find out how other elementary principals felt about achievement testing, I gave a survey asking principals to respond to a number of statements. The 10-item survey sampled the views of principals from two large, diverse school districts — the Las Vegas district and an anonymous district in the South. It addressed the validity of achievement testing for young children, the pressure surrounding testing, and the effects of testing on classroom practices. I asked the principals to agree or disagree with various statements.

The first two statements on the survey read: "Achievement tests are generally valid for assessing what children learn in grades K–2," and "Achievement tests are generally valid for assessing what students learn in grades 3–12." Forty-seven percent of the Las Vegas principals and 68% of the southern school district's principals agreed that achievement tests are valid for assessing what K–2 children learn. A greater number in both surveys supported the validity of achievement tests for older children. Although the survey indicates that many principals question the validity of achievement testing for young children, it also demonstrates that many others need to learn what to look for besides specific bits of knowledge (see Chapters 11 and 13).

Regarding the pressure to produce higher test scores, 54% of the Las Vegas respondents indicated that they felt this pressure. The two main sources of pressure identified were parent/community and press/

media. The survey conducted in the southern school district produced significantly different findings: 95% of the principals felt pressure to produce higher test scores. The main source of pressure they identified was the central office administration. The Las Vegas experience with excessively high test scores and the resultant efforts of the school board and central office to reduce feelings of pressure seem to be reflected in the outcome of the survey. The findings from the southern school district probably reflect more accurately the feelings of principals across the nation and the pressure involved in the looking-good game.

The third area covered in the survey was the effect of achievement testing on classroom practices. Statements that dealt specifically with this area were: (1) "Achievement tests affect classroom practices in K–2," (2) "Achievement tests have harmful effects on K–2 classroom practices," and (3) "Achievement tests lead to an emphasis on skills instruction rather than on thinking, meaning, curiosity, and/or inventiveness." Eighty-two percent of the Las Vegas principals and 96% of the southern district's principals agreed that achievement tests affect classroom practices in K–2. Fifty-three percent and 43% respectively agreed that the effects were harmful. In response to the third item, 91% of the Las Vegas respondents and 81% of the principals in the South agreed that tests lead to an emphasis on skills rather than on thinking, meaning, curiosity, and/or inventiveness.

Finally, more than half of the principals in both surveys expressed support for a halt to paper-and-pencil achievement tests for young children.

An aspect of testing that I could have included in the survey is the effect of testing on the socioemotional climate of the school. As an elementary school principal, I dread the time of year when it is once again time to give the tests. It seems that no matter how hard I work to downplay the importance of testing, I observe teacher's anxieties escalating. As teachers become anxious, so do children. I have come to expect that during test week teachers will be on edge and that there will be an increased number of children in the nurse's office with headaches and stomach aches.

I remember walking through a classroom during test week and observing a small boy crying. I asked him what was wrong, and he replied, "I didn't mark all the little circles and now I can't go to third grade." I knew the idea of "pass" or "fail" has not come from the teacher; in fact the teacher had worked hard to alleviate fears. Yet for the young boy the idea of not passing was real. As explained in Chapter 2, children are not empty containers who merely internalize what we tell them.

One good way to assess children's learning is to interact with them and observe their thinking processes. A skillful teacher gains much more insight into children's thinking by studying their behavior than by glancing at the results of tests that only touch upon fragments of what they can do intellectually.

In an era when there seems to be a desire to create instructional settings that foster thinking, meaning, curiosity, and inventiveness, we are giving tests that we know do not measure these qualities. A far more appropriate way to assess children's learning is to interact with them and observe their thinking processes. A skillful teacher gains much more insight into children's thinking by studying their behaviors. Testing puts teachers' insights and knowledge down instead of inspiring them to learn more about children's thinking.

What principals can do

Principals are supposedly in key positions as instructional leaders of their schools, but the leadership has clearly shifted to a million-dollar testing industry. Following are some of the things principals can do to lead early childhood education forward rather than being led backward to the "basics" as defined by the testing industry.

Educating ourselves. Only half of the principals in Las Vegas and one-third of those surveyed in the South stated that achievement tests are not valid in grades K–2. While nearly all of them said that achievement tests affect classroom practices, only half thought their effects were harmful. These findings suggest that more principals need to become knowledgeable about how children learn and how we can tell whether or not children are learning.

Through organizations such as the National Association of Elementary School Principals and its local affiliates, we can request help in in-service education. As *Improving the Preparation of School Administrators: An Agenda for Reform* (National Policy Board for Educational Administration, 1989) states, administrators must better understand the process of teaching and learning.

Educating our staff. If each principal carried out a strong and coherent in-service staff development program, teachers would become convinced that young children learn by interacting meaningfully with objects and people. Principals can organize study groups and committees to solve specific problems, such as devising better report cards. We can also facilitate teachers' observations of each other's classrooms so that they can grow in practice as well as in theoretical understanding of learning and development.

When principals are convinced that children learn when they are intrigued and deeply interested in an activity, they can usually find many ways of encouraging teachers to grow in the same direction. Staff development takes many years. Educating and hiring good student teachers is another way to add new blood and knowledge to the staff. Teachers who are strong in theory stand up to justify their practices.

Educating parents. Parents often put pressure on teachers to produce higher test scores and to use worksheets. A principal can plan meetings to explain to parents why test scores are misleading and how test-driven instruction stifles children's thinking. Parents want the best for their children, and many are grateful to be told that drilling children leads only to the illusion of learning.

Educating the media. Reporters often ask principals, especially around the time test scores come out, how they plan to use the test results. These are opportunities to educate reporters, who greatly influence public opinion. Some free-lance reporters are beginning to write about the negative effects of testing, but most journalists speak and write as if tests infallibly reveal the whole truth and the final truth about children's learning.

Changing the laws and regulations mandating achievement testing. The testing bandwagon is too loud and too powerful for individual principals to fight alone. It is, therefore, necessary to work through professional organizations to educate legislators and local and state school boards to ban standardized achievement testing in grades K–2. The organizations already advocating this position are the National Association for the Education of Young Children (1988a, 1988b), the National Association of Elementary School Principals (1989), the Association for Supervision and Curriculum Development (1987), the National Association of Early Childhood Teacher Educators (1989), the National Council of Teachers of English (1989), the National Council of Teachers of Mathematics (1989), and the Association for Childhood Education International (Perrone, 1977).

Teachers and principals are in close contact with children and daily feel the detrimental effects of achievement testing. Rather than continuing to comply with mandates that create only illusions of reform, principals and teachers must start to redirect the reform movement. Change from within is the only way to achieve lasting improvement in an individual or a group.

Chapter 6

The Dilemma for Teachers

Christine Chaillé and Linda Barber

Over the past several years, as improvement of the nation's schools has come to the public's attention, the underlying message accompanying the testing mandate has become stronger and stronger: "You will provide a program that will promote high scores on the achievement test." How do teachers translate this mandate and its underlying message? How do teachers respond when the emphasis on achievement testing forces them to do things that conflict with what they believe is good education? How does the achievement testing mandate affect teachers' feelings of autonomy and decision making, and how does that translate into teachers' motivation to teach and what they do with children in the classroom?

At the same time that the testing mania is strangling the educational system nationwide, there is *another* viewpoint, another position, that is rapidly gaining advocates. This is the belief that learning experiences for 5-, 6-, and 7-year-olds should be developmentally appropriate (Bredekamp, 1987), and that there are more effective ways of assessing learning than by an excessive amount of standardized testing (NAEYC, 1988a). On which side of the debate should the teachers of young children be?

This chapter will deal with the teacher's perspective on these issues. In oral and written testimony, many teachers of young children have conveyed to us their experiences with and reactions to standardized testing. From this testimony, we have identified common concerns teachers share. To highlight these issues we begin with accounts from two teachers and end with the direction in which teachers can act to end the interplay of the looking-good and keep-my-job games.

One teacher, whom we will call Mary, is from a district currently using standardized tests for all grades. The other teacher, whom we will call Joyce, has experienced such a district but is now in a very different situation.

Two teachers cope with the keep-my-job game

Mary says:

Like most teachers, I have had a variety of feelings in connection with achievement testing—anxiety, anger, frustration, and resignation. Many factors contributed to these feelings.

For instance, achievement tests seemed to cause a different kind of anxiety for me as a beginning teacher compared to when I had become an experienced teacher. As a beginning, untenured teacher I definitely felt that my job was in jeopardy if my students didn't test well. As an experienced teacher, my concern lies more with the appropriateness of the test and what consequences achievement testing holds for children.

Originally our district tested in the spring. This changed about four years ago, when our district went to fall testing. Spring testing seemed to have more effect on my teaching. I felt as if *I* were being tested as much as the children. I would make sure that I covered with more emphasis the types of problems that were on the test, often giving work to the children in the format they would see on the test. I justified this by telling myself that I was just making it easier for children to get past the pressure of the testing situation. Not that this wasn't true, but it was also because I wanted to make sure that they did well.

As I taught longer, I began to resent this pressure. I thought I was doing a good job and did not need to prepare children for the test. But even though I would talk a big game about ignoring the upcoming tests, as they came close, I became less confident. I would watch other teachers as they made sure they covered everything that was on the test and would succumb to my fears: "What if my children don't do as well? They'll really be at a disadvantage if the other teachers are priming their students." Then I would have to deal with my weakness and would question my "real" ability as a teacher. It seemed to me that a good teacher should not have to provide anything beyond a regular program—therefore, I was not a good teacher.

I would prepare the children the month before testing. I often felt unprofessional in doing this. Even though I was confident (I thought) in my program, which tended to be more experiential than a typical academic program, I was concerned that, if my children didn't do well, I would be forced to make changes in my classroom.

Testing is one of the things that has driven a wedge between me and my district. There are numerous ways my district treats its teachers that remove any feeling of professionalism or autonomy. Testing has been one of the most dramatic for me. We have become adversaries rather than partners with common goals. The district uses the results of tests, which take place over three or four days, without regard to teacher judgment. There are so many factors to consider beyond the limiting capacity of achievement tests. Then it uses these narrow results to judge a teacher's program. It's positively maddening.

Although echoing Mary's conflicts, Joyce's description of the struggles she has had over many years in a variety of schools and school districts ends on a more positive note.

Joyce says:

I have had a variety of experiences with testing. I've found as I've become more educated about testing and as I feel stronger about my own beliefs—that testing is basically harmless and is such a small part of what I do—it doesn't intimidate me.

I can remember being intimidated. When I was a beginning teacher, they published the results of the district test scores in the paper. It was pretty obvious how each class at my school scored. At that time I took testing very seriously and felt any low scores were a direct reflection of my poor teaching. But my classes there scored well on tests and I was deemed a successful teacher on that basis.

As I moved to other buildings and my students began to score lower, I found each principal handled it a little differently. My level of concern somewhat depended on how important test scores were to the principal.

I did not appreciate the negative feedback on the results of the tests each year. It was given in a negative, punitive manner. It became ridiculous to me when we had to spend hours devising strategies to improve test scores.

About this time I began to get "test smart." It was obvious the tests did not test our curriculum and were very limiting in what they could tell me about my children. I began to view the test process as an irritation and an interruption from the real teaching.

Now I'm in a different district. I have recently taken an assessment class and it confirmed the hunches I have had all along about tests. The district paid for this class. It wants to help teachers assume an active role in assessing students in ways besides standardized tests. Kindergarten and first grade children do not take tests here. The debate continues, but the teachers pushed for that and presented a good enough argument that the board agreed. It does want some assessing of students but wants teachers to assume some responsibility in doing that. The board also gives you time off and pays for you to pursue that goal! It's a totally different concept to be in an environment where we are treated so professionally.

As can be seen in these two accounts, the dilemma for teachers centers around some common issues that interconnect. These issues include: (1) what and how to teach, (2) teacher motivation, and (3) children's motivation to learn.

What and how to teach

Educational programs should focus on the development of the whole child. Primary grade teachers from Early Childhood and Progressive Education backgrounds have a long tradition of using curriculum activities that promote creativity, social interaction, and problem solving along with knowledge and skill acquisition (for example, see Kamii & DeVries, 1980; Hirsch, 1984; Barbour, Webster, & Drosdeck, 1987; Hubbard, 1987, 1988; Connell, 1987; Sawyers & Rogers, 1988; Tudge & Caruso, 1988; Holt, 1989; Nachbar, 1989). Achievement tests, however, emphasize one area of a child's development, the intellectual, and that in a fragmented and narrowly defined way (see Chapter 2). The tests' narrow "academic" emphasis, in turn, encourages teachers to focus on narrowly defined, isolated, surface "skills," and to spend disproportionate amounts of time in activities that promote the learning of these skills. This often comes at the expense of other aspects of children's development — social, emotional, creative, and physical, for example — as activities that promote these aspects are often left out for lack of time.

Methods that promote chances for success on the test often work against the construction of real knowledge. These test-aligned methods include:

- Lots of paper-and-pencil work. This often takes the place of interactions with real objects and people, interactions that young children need in order to learn.
- Lots of drill and practice activities. These emphasize two things that work against meaningful intellectual activity — speed and the one right answer.
- Convergent, as opposed to divergent, problem solving. Right-wrong, black-white types of problems and situations are emphasized in tests, where there is little opportunity for exploration of alternatives, multiple possibilities, or predictions.
- Lack of attention to individual differences and styles. Each child is expected to do the same thing in the same way at the same time, which

does not acknowledge the diversity of what children are bringing to the educational setting and their different styles of learning.

Effects of testing on teacher motivation

Many of the teachers who shared their experiences with us commented on the effects of the hypocritical stance they are forced into by giving tests that they do not believe in. "The way that achievement testing compromises me is the fact that I have to give them at all. Achievement tests violate everything I believe in with regard to working with young children."

Other teachers expressed anguish at seeing children struggle and at having children cry because they felt like failures. One teacher, for example, said that the most negative effect on her was "seeing the children become frustrated and hearing comments like 'I'm dumb,' and 'I can't do this.'" Another teacher said that she tries to make the test a "challenge" activity, one that is no big deal, but "I've had kids cry. If there's one child that is discouraged or disheartened, I get furious. If they handle it, I'm OK."

Using young children's test scores to evaluate teachers

The practice of using test scores as part of a teacher's evaluation also affects teachers' motivation. This practice seems to vary according to districts' policies and principals' beliefs. One teacher we spoke to was put on probation at least in part because of her students' low test scores, and the low performance was made known to the other teachers. "I felt the most pressure from my peers. I did not want any of them to feel as though I was not capable of teaching first grade."

Teachers report that in some districts there are policies that invoke "decision rules" based on a teacher's class scores (their distance from the national mean). A decision 1 means the class scores are acceptable, and decision 2 means you should take note but no specific plan is required. If you get a decision 3 or 4, it means your program needs to be changed to bring up the scores, and the district requires it be done in a specified way. If, for example, your first graders did not do well on the fall test (as beginning second graders), the district requires that you outline and show how you will implement a program that will overcome the "deficiencies." The district sees decision rules as program evaluation tools, but the teacher's plan to "fix" her program, with the goal of

Ignoring the teacher's considerable knowledge of each child, and relying only on standardized tests to make major judgments about the child's life, insults the teacher. Many teachers feel punished by these tests —punished for good teaching, which does not align exactly with the peculiar test items, but results in a better education for the child.

subsequently raising test scores, becomes a part of her job performance evaluation. Whether districts intend scores as formal teacher evaluation criteria or not, many teachers perceive themselves as evaluated by their children's test performance.

"The pressure comes from administrators when we are forced to work under decision rules. The children's individual growth isn't as important as how the whole district compares nationally on tests. It's always been very demoralizing to me." Even more frustrating to teachers in such districts is that most often the decision 3s and 4s are in the schools with very transient, low socioeconomic populations. In some cases, the population that takes the test in the fall is a very different population than was in the program the preceding spring; yet teachers are evaluated on those children's scores.

"Most teachers feel very punished by decision rules. They spend a lot of time planning how to raise test scores, which often includes rote methods of teaching, not how to make the children better thinkers or problem solvers, nor how to make learning interesting or meaningful. That's the bottom line. High scores make the district look good and make for good public relations, which in turn helps to pass school budgets. Test scores are tangible black and white proof that we know what we're doing."

Evaluation of teacher performance using children's test scores lessens teacher motivation. "When the decision 3 was invoked, I had to make a plan to 'beef-up' my curriculum. My plan needed to be coordinated with the other second grade teacher and written in proposal form. The proposal was turned in to the principal, who, in turn, gave it to the higher ups. After the proposal was accepted, it was assumed that I would follow the plan. Consequently, I covered myself by including proposal ideas in my weekly plans. This was a waste of time because I did it only to cover myself, and it led to anger and resentment about what it implied about my professional judgment. In reality, my values and beliefs cannot be compromised. After doing a little timed testing, I said, 'Forget it; this doesn't make sense. I'll just pretend to follow my written plans to keep the principal off my back.' "

Effects of testing on children's motivation

A diet of drill and worksheets cannot inspire children to be interested in schoolwork. Most young children come to school with a natural desire to learn, but faced with such a diet lose interest. For many it is a time of particularly intense and important socialization. The quality of children's first school experiences has a significant effect on their general outlook on school and learning and on how they face later school experiences.

One first grade teacher described what she observed: "Many parents make statements such as 'You've got to get to bed early tonight, tomorrow's the big test'; 'You have to do well on the test if you want to stay in first grade'; 'If you do well on the test, we'll buy you a new . . . .' "

Neither parents nor children know that achievement tests are made so that 50% of the pupils will come out below the mean.

She goes on: "While a few handle their inability to answer questions relatively well, some react with tears, others with bad behavior, still others with withdrawal—probably the most dangerous behavior."

What teachers can do

As teachers, we find ourselves caught in an educational system that puts excessive emphasis on accountability as measured by test scores. What can individual teachers who feel professionally and ethically slighted because of standardized tests do to change the system?

We believe that teachers can do a great deal (see Seefeldt & Barbour, 1988). The controversy over testing and developmentally appropriate education is attracting much attention as different groups—researchers, teacher educators, parents, *and* classroom teachers—voice their concerns. This increased attention presents an opportunity for teachers who share views about the misuse of standardized testing to join together. First, teachers, like those in Joyce's district, must feel strongly enough to begin the work of stopping the testing surge. Many teachers who have concerns over testing may feel that the problem is somehow unique to their classroom. Often-isolated teachers may not have the time or ability to obtain the research and resources that can validate their concerns. By joining together, teachers can share their concerns about testing and ideas about alternatives to it. Strength comes with unification, and voices joined together are heard.

Once teachers have a clear voice, they can reach out to administrators, school boards, parents, and politicians. How that is done may vary depending on the community. More information sharing and dialogue in both informal and formal situations can help clarify the issues involved in testing. Educators and parents are most likely to be concerned and to talk about the negative effects of standardized testing. Others who do not deal with children daily may need more convincing evidence about the negative effects of testing on classroom practices. In marshalling evidence and resources, teachers can draw on state and national groups, such as NAEYC, that have compiled information for just such purposes.

In some districts, the most difficult to convince are those who wield the most control: the administrators and school board members. Wit-

Teachers of young children can become members of one or another professional association that is strongly against so much narrow academic skill testing, and such inappropriate curriculum in kindergarten and first and second grades. Those with the same concerns can band together and inform themselves by reading the vast amount of material being published today on this subject: progressive educational reform in the early grades.

ness the differences teacher input made in the two districts described earlier by Mary and Joyce, differences that are typical. Many districts view policymaking as an administrative task that does not involve teacher judgment. Teachers in such districts will have to be even more determined and more diplomatic, often rallying parents to carry the information and arguments forward to those who make decisions.

Acknowledge and advocate for *appropriate* assessment. Within the classroom and school, individual teachers have the task of implementing and polishing alternative methods of assessment (see Chapters 11 and 13) and of sharing those alternatives with others. Let parents know the meaning and uses of developmentally appropriate assessment techniques. Collaborate and share with colleagues, and keep administrators informed on the alternatives and their rationale.

While the work to make changes in testing is occurring, teachers still have the weighty responsibility of guiding young children through standardized tests with as little negative effect as possible. Teachers can lessen the threat of testing for children by keeping their classroom programs consistent throughout the year. Tests should not be allowed to disrupt the confidence that the children have gained. This means that teachers must have faith in their programs. Through individual and collective action, teachers can participate in resolving the dilemma that they are faced with in contending with standardized testing.

Chapter 7

The Dilemma for Teacher Educators

Anne G. Dorsey

Should I teach my college students what I know is best for young children, or should I tailor my courses to what currently exists in many public schools? Should I look the other way when the student teachers I supervise perpetuate practices that stifle children's thinking? These are the dilemmas I face every day. If I prepare teachers to fit into the test-driven schools, I am playing the looking-good game and the buck-passing game. Perhaps I need to convince myself that future teachers should be able to use both the best approach *and* the one that is now driven by external demands. However, it is hard enough to learn to be a teacher without such complications.

As an early childhood teacher educator, I am aware that although state and local curriculum committees *appear* to determine the public school curriculum, it is the questions on standardized achievement tests that in reality play the influential role. The evaluation of a school's overall instructional program is now based primarily on standardized test scores.

My student teachers often come to see me and say in effect, "My cooperating teacher is great. [A cooperating teacher is a teacher who agrees to let a student teacher practice-teach in her or his classroom.] She believes all the things we have learned about good activities for children. But she said she can't do them because the children have to be ready for the test." When I hear this, I face a dilemma.

What should I teach future teachers?

When children are going to be given standardized achievement tests, teachers often focus on the types of information and skills that are on the test. (See Chapter 6.) I could simply teach college students how to teach specific bits of knowledge through direct instructon. If so, my job would be easy. When the authors of textbooks and workbooks have already made the decisions about what the children will learn, neither teachers nor children need to think, and direct instruction of specific fragments does produce higher test scores.

Somewhere *the decision to use or not to use standardized achievement tests with kindergarten and primary grade children is made by human beings; the questions on the tests are not truly in control of the instructional program in the classroom.*

However, I believe on the basis of research and scientific theory that young children learn best when they have many opportunities to interact with peers, to share and defend their ideas, to play, and to pursue their own interests. I know that workbooks and most drill and practice exercises waste time and deprive children of opportunities to be intrigued about phenomena and ideas. I teach my students how children construct knowledge. I help them learn to listen to and observe children and to guide their learning by providing a wide range of interesting materials and ideas to explore. I value the child's autonomy and view both children and teachers as learners. Both children and teachers must become able to make their own decisions about right and wrong and about true and false. Learning only to obey and to follow is not education.

What do other teacher educators think?

To ascertain how other college professors facing this quandary are responding, I mailed an Early Childhood Teacher Educator's Survey (Dorsey, 1988) to 300 members of the National Association of Early Childhood Teacher Educators. Some members of the organizaton prepare students only for preschool teaching and may, therefore, have chosen not to respond. Of the 137 responding, 136 said they prepare students for teaching in kindergarten and the primary grades.

Early childhood education faculty appear to have a fair degree of control over what they teach in college early childhood education classes. As reported in the survey, content of early childhood education courses is determined primarily by the instructor (30%) and by group decision of the early education faculty (36%). However, 32% of the respondents reported that certification requirements guided what they teach. I asked the teacher educators to rank other factors that influenced the content of early childhood education courses. The program philsophy carried heavy weight, as did the instructor's philosophy. Early childhood education professors described their philosophy as one that focused on children's experience rather than on memorization, on long-term rather than short-term goals, and on process rather than on product. The importance of the child's self-esteem and the responsibility of the teacher to avoid unnecessary stress on children were frequently mentioned, as was emphasis on the teacher's teaching based on her observation of each child's development. These professors supported the position that teachers often must make complex judgments and that "teaching expertise is not acquired through the accumulation of mimetic knowledge (prescriptions of what to do); instead, it develops when teachers have learned *how to decide* what to do" (Kennedy, 1987, p. 143).

In examining the opinion of the survey respondents, it is clear that these early childhood teacher educators believe that standardized achievement testing in kindergarten and the primary grades is not only useless but also detrimental to children. Seventy-three percent said that standardized tests in these grades do not measure effectively what children learn.

When asked to list three things they would like to change about standardized testing of 5-, 6-, and 7-year-olds, the great majority of early childhood teacher educators wrote in one way or another that the tests should be eliminated or that less classroom time should be spent on them.

What happens in student teaching?

No matter what professors teach, college students encounter a variety of circumstances when they enter public school classrooms for observation or student teaching. Some schools are inspiring; others are demoralizing. Early childhood professors, of course, seek excellent teachers to be the models for their students while they practice-teach. They look for teachers who understand and act on their knowledge of current theory about how children learn. Such teachers, however, are not readily available.

Student teachers often find practices that require children to complete every page of the basal reader, the accompanying workbook, and the math workbook. The student who has been taught to plan based on children's interests and ways of learning may become confused and perhaps feel betrayed by her college professors if she feels unprepared for the "real world." She may find it difficult or impossible to meet her cooperating teacher's expectations.

Faced with these concerns, I have to address the "survival" issue both in terms of coaching students in classroom management and in terms of helping them develop curriculum. While not necessarily ideal, the college curriculum must bridge the chasm between the lockstep worksheet approach and the constructivist approach described in Chapter 2. I first focus on the scientific and theoretical basis for the approach to teaching and learning which I espouse. If I fail to do this, students are left to rely on what "works." What "works" usually means short-term, superficial solutions that give the misleading impression of success.

One student teacher was told by her second grade cooperating teacher to teach a social studies lesson about maps. The teacher added, however, that only the children who finished their work could do the activity the student had designed. Finishing their work meant reading the chapter aloud round-robin style and writing all the end-of-chapter questions and answers. The student teacher's activity consisted of making maps and examining maps she and the children had brought in. The assigned work was a long text that was boring and unrelated to the children's experiences. Many whispered or surreptitiously examined items in their desks. A constant parade left for the restroom, and those who did not finish the assignment were not allowed to go out for recess. The supplies for map making lay untouched on the student teacher's desk as did the maps that the children had brought.

Dismayed, the student discussed her lesson with the teacher. The explanation she received was that on the test the children would not be asked to draw a map or to look at complicated maps such as a Florida road map, which a child had brought from a recent trip. Instead they would be asked questions similar to those in the text. The teacher felt it would be inappropriate to use valuable social studies time for an "extra" activity. She told the student teacher to write children's names on the board when they whispered to induce them to behave more appropriately and to let her concentrate on teaching.

The student teacher felt frustrated. She had put all her energy into group management and little into the learning process. She felt unsuccessful at both. During her conference with me, the goal she set for herself was the improvement of her management skills. The student could not see that the management problem could be prevented, at least in part, by activities in which children were interested. Even if she had understood this basic idea, how could she have implemented it in the student teaching situation if her cooperating teacher did not want her to?

I face situations such as this regularly. Should I tell the student that the teacher was correct in stressing the importance of covering all the text material? I don't think I should; I think I should sympathize with the student teacher (it's too bad she is in this double-bind situation) and help her understand why the teacher does as she does. I think I should also tell the student that her idea was a good one, that she should tactfully keep trying to teach her own ways, and that she should plan to have the most constructivist classroom possible when she has her *own* classroom in the future. Besides, we have to maintain working relationships with the schools, since future teachers cannot be prepared without the cooperation of school personnel. Perhaps most important, change is unlikely to occur unless educators in many roles—teacher educators, classroom teachers, and many others—work together to bring it about.

When asked to list three things they would like to change about standardized testing of 5-, 6-, and 7-year-olds, the great majority of early childhood teacher educators wrote in one way or another that the tests should be eliminated or that less classroom time should be spent on them. The teacher educators surveyed, almost all of whom prepare kindergarten and primary teachers, believe in developmentally appropriate classrooms that foster intellectual autonomy for teachers and children.

What happens after student teaching?

The dilemma does not end on the last day of student teaching. Students face it during job interviews when they are asked about their opinion of behaviorist approaches. Interviewers have often been schooled in the behaviorist approach and believe strongly in the value of standardized tests for young children. Prospective teachers who do not provide agreeable answers to questions about teaching phonics, drilling math facts, and managing a quiet, teacher-centered classroom will almost certainly be passed over by the principal who supports those approaches. It is not helpful for a university professor to say that one wouldn't want to work for that kind of administrator anyway and to encourage the student to wait for a position in a school that values the development of autonomy in children.

Similar problems face the beginning teacher who is ostracized by experienced "direct instruction" teachers. Seasoned teachers sometimes deride the beginner for her theoretical approach and for the intensity with which she seeks to learn about the children in her class. Thus isolated, the newcomer may become discouraged and decide to conform to the norm of direct instruction or to drop out of teaching.

What professors can do

1. Professors can work to improve the quality of colleges of education by ensuring that they are preparing future teachers *and* future administrators with the knowledge they will need to put appropriate programs in place in their schools. We must recognize that the teachers and administrators who are now in schools over-using standardized tests came from our colleges and universities and may not have been given opportunities to learn in depth about more appropriate approaches to working with young children. Students may have been taught the right theory, but not given enough practical experience (on the campus) in actually *implementing* it.

2. Professors can ensure that their students are well grounded in knowledge of a variety of ways to assess children's learning and that they know the limitations of achievement tests.

3. Professors must prepare students for the arguments they will hear from colleagues, parents, and administrators, and be sure that they know the counter-arguments, too.

4. Professors must contribute to and keep current with the research literature about the inadequacy of achievement tests and behaviorist teaching so that they can provide the necessary resources to their students and work effectively with school districts. The academic freedom that professors enjoy allows them to speak out in a reasoned way.

5. Professors can work to develop a larger pool of well-qualified cooperating teachers. This may be done, in part, through providing in-service programs. However, a more far-reaching program would require becoming involved in the school reform movement. This approach provides differentiated staffing, so that several student teachers and several in-service teachers could work under the guidance of a master teacher.

6. Professors can build networks with effective teachers and can invite those teachers to address their classes or team teach college classes. They can request opportunities for college students to observe effective teachers in their kindergarten or primary grade classroom. Many teachers would welcome a connection with others who support the developmentally appropriate work they are attempting to do, often under difficult circumstances.

7. Professors can work to link prospective teachers with knowledgeable principals who will encourage them to use what they know to be good practice and will not require them to participate in inappropriate teaching and testing methods. Later these teachers can become mentors for other teachers.

8. Professors can organize courses and in-service development programs to help principals and other administrators learn recommended early childhood education practice, so that they can encourage teachers trying to create constructivist, developmentally appropriate learning experiences for 5- to 7-year-old children.

9. Professors can form statewide networks to disseminate information to one another and to school boards, administrators, and legislators. Organizations such as the National Association of Early Childhood Teacher Educators and its affiliates can play a strong leadership role here.

10. Professors can write articles and participate in media interviews in order to reach the public. Parents are eager to provide the best for their children. Taxpayers want their tax dollars used wisely. By reaching the public with reasoned arguments, professors can de-

velop a pool of community supporters who will advocate appropriate teaching/testing policies.

11. Professors can work to change laws and regulations mandating standardized testing in the early grades. NAEYC and its Affiliates have a strong model for obtaining and disseminating legislative information. Professors can contribute to that network and encourage others to participate also. They can teach their college students to keep informed about the legislative process and about current issues and encourage them to make their opinions and information known to their legislators.

Teacher educators can provide courses in constructivist, developmentally appropriate education for young children to students, teachers, and administrators. They can participate in educating the public as to what all this is about and help people develop an understanding of sensible assessment of children's progress.

12. Finally, because beginning teachers need a long time to construct knowledge about the constructivist approach and about the detrimental effects of programs driven by standardized tests, teacher educators must continue to provide opportunities for continued growth. When universities provide a solid grounding in constructivist theory, along with realistic examples of classroom practices, future teachers are more likely to make the effort to think about their practice in relation to constructivism.

Teacher educators *must* recognize that we have the opportunity to take a leadership role. In no other profession are obsolete methods taught side-by-side with current practice as though they were of equal worth. We must teach our students from our knowledge base, using the research data we have. We cannot expect children to learn to think from teachers whose preparation avoided this most potent approach to learning.

Chapter 8

The Dilemma for State Department Consultants

Steven J. Leinwand

A large part of my job entails conducting teacher in-service sessions designed to help improve the quality of mathematics instruction in schools and districts. It is typical to begin a session by addressing the need to change *what* we have been teaching as well as *how* we have been teaching. We often discuss the importance of problem solving and the development of number sense. With teachers of primary grade children, I address the need for a developmentally appropriate curriculum that builds mathematical understanding through extensive use of concrete materials and pictures.

But then, usually from the back of the room, right after discussion of a sample activity, comes the question that has been growing gradually in everyone's mind: "I agree with what you're saying. It makes a lot of sense, but what about our achievement tests?"

As I have noted before (Leinwand, 1986):

> This is the critical question in any discussion of curricular change. The frequency with which it arises underscores the pervasive influence of these tests on what gets taught. The question expresses the underlying fear of daring to omit topics that appear on these tests. It also reminds us that in most schools standardized test results are the single most important measure of educational success in the eyes of the administration, the parents, the community, and the media. This being the case, most teachers make every reasonable effort to prepare their students for this content. In this fashion, standardized testing programs, more than texts or local or state curricula, drive mathematics instruction and serve as the greatest single obstacle to the implementation of positive change. (p. 3)

As curriculum supervisors and facilitators of instructional improvement, we thus increasingly find ourselves in binds that compromise what we know is best for children. This difficult situation gnaws away at reform efforts and undermines the very improvements that tests were instituted to foster in the first place.

Major organizations of math experts call for less memorization and more understanding

In mathematics, we have a broad-based consensus on the elements of an effective mathematics program in an age of calculators and computers. *This consensus, responsive to changing societal needs and demands for workers who can think, advocates more reasoning and less memorization, more estimation and mental arithmetic, and less paper-and-pencil computation.* Educators trying to achieve this goal by implementing a constructivist or developmentally appropriate progam for young children become increasingly frustrated. On the one hand, they see leaders in education becoming clearer and more united on the direction of curricular revision, but, on the other, they see teachers finding it harder and harder to implement such revisions because of the demands of the standardized testing system pressing upon us.

The basic thrust of the curriculum reform effort in mathematics is best summarized in the National Council of Teachers of Mathematics' *Curriculum and Evaluation Standards for School Mathematics* (1989), which calls for "a shift in emphasis from a curriculum dominated by memorization of isolated facts and procedures and proficiency with paper-and-pencil skills, to one that emphasizes conceptual understandings, multiple representations and connections, and mathematical problem solving" (p. 125).

This call for a change in direction is echoed in the Mathematical Sciences Education Board's draft "A Framework for Revision of K–12 Mathematics Curricula" (Mathematical Sciences Education Board, 1988), the basic premise of which is

> that a major restructuring of the content of K–12 mathematics in the United States is needed if the mathematics education our children receive is to give them the knowledge—and the ability to use that knowledge—that they will require to be personally and professionally competent in the twenty-first century. (p. 2)

Frustration arises when, because of standardized tests, the critical "shift in emphasis" and "restructuring" remain an unattainable vision for all too many teachers and their pupils. Who has the time to make

The National Council of Teachers of Mathematics, the Mathematical Sciences Education Board, and other major groups are calling for less memorization, less paper-and-pencil computation, and more reasoning, estimation, and mental arithmetic because of changes in today's world. But standardized tests still reward the wrong things (and punish the right things) in terms of society's current needs. Teachers are very reluctant to change their way of teaching math to young children because they do not want them to do poorly on the all-important tests.

problem solving a daily focus when so much of the test measures computation and mathematical vocabulary and symbolism? Who can dare incorporate calculators into classroom instruction when these instruments are barred from use on the standardized tests? Who can risk shifting focus to broad conceptual understandings in the face of tests that assess little more than rote procedural knowledge?

In these ways, standardized tests, used to respond to simplistic and expedient notions of accountability within an incredibly complex enterprise, quickly come to dominate our entire educational landscape. Nowhere is this situation more destructive than in the primary grades.

The mechanics of the vote-getting, looking-good, and buck-passing games

Why do tests have such influence? Consider the process played out annually in school districts across the nation. Most parents and school board members assume that standardized tests are objective and scientific measures of educational quality. In fact, school board members do not really understand how standardized tests are developed, nor how limited they are. Representing the community at large in overseeing the increasingly expensive educational enterprise, lay school board members expect test scores to continually improve. Thus they commonly adopt an understandably narrow view that is best summarized as: "Get those test scores up to where they should be."

As I described elsewhere (Leinwand, 1985), the ensuing process, common to school districts across the country, goes as follows:

> The day after the board meeting at the obligatory "morning-after-the-board-meeting" staff meeting, the superintendent tells the assembled principals that "the board is extremely concerned about the low math scores." In turn, on the following Monday afternoon, at each obligatory "Monday-after-the-staff-meeting" faculty meeting, each principal tells the assembled teachers that "the board and the central office are extremely concerned that we boost those math scores." (p. 26)

So begins a conspiracy of good intentions that inexorably shifts our attention from children to percentiles, from a broad education to narrow skills, and from thinking and reasoning to remembering and regurgitating. The looking-good game is being played with great intensity and considerable anxiety by all.

Teachers soon succumb to the pressures of test mania. Aware of the content of the tests, they make every reasonable effort to prepare their kindergartners and first and second graders for the types of items found on the test. Thus it is that in most schools standardized tests drive the instructional program in reading, language arts, and mathematics.

Illustrative items from a standardized math test

To better understand the destructive force of most standardized tests, one must turn to specific test items. Here one finds multiple-choice, right-wrong items that assess memorization far more than understanding, and rote learning of isolated rules and procedures far more than integrated processes and connections. Three examples from the mathematics subtest of a major standardized test illustrate the problem.

Example 1. In an item on a test recommended for grades 1.5 to 2.9, the teacher says: "Mark under the symbol that makes the sentence true." The question in the children's test booklet is similar to the one shown in Figure 8.1. Items like this are typical of the mathematical concepts subtest. On the surface, such items look reasonable enough. However, if a first grader gets it wrong, this is usually because the $>$ and $<$ signs are confusing. If we simply ask first graders to circle the larger number, most of them have no trouble. Unfortunately, such an item never appears on the test either because too many children get the correct answer or because it does not allow for three or four choices and optical scanning machine scoring. As a result of such items, teachers are forced to focus instruction on excessive drill of this kind of superficial knowledge.

Figure 8.1
An Example of a Multiple-Choice Test Item

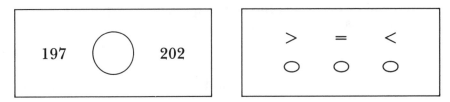

Example 2. In another item, the teacher says: "Mark the expanded numeral for 132." The choices in the child's test booklet are similar to the following four:

○ $1 + 3 + 2$
○ $1 + 3 + 20$
○ $13 + 2 + 10$
○ $100 + 30 + 2$

Again, this seems like a reasonable enough item on the surface, but such items foster exactly the kind of mindless paper-and-pencil drill that least helps children develop their mathematical understanding. Since this is how children's understanding of place value is assessed, teachers are rarely encouraged to use the base ten materials that allow children to develop real understanding of place value.

To make matters even worse, it is possible that an administrator, desperate to raise test scores, would misinterpret the item by thinking that it involves sums of two and three digit numbers and demands that this skill, totally inappropriately, now be added to the first grade curriculum.

Example 3. Another typical item is illustrative of the premature abstraction of the material and the related acceleration of the curriculum. The teacher says aloud: "Mark to show which is the least amount of money." Then, rather than showing pictures of coins, which the teacher has been using as a developmentally appropriate tool for money skills, including skip counting (5, 10, 15) and addition, the child's test booklet lists the following numerals and words:

○ 4   nickels
○ 21 pennies
○ 3   dimes
○ 1   quarter

Young children *can* answer this kind of question with coins but tend to get the test answer wrong because

1. being allowed to move coins makes thinking much easier for young children, and
2. 4×5, $5 + 5 + 5 + 5$, 3×10, and $10 + 10 + 10$ are not yet part of the curriculum.

When many children fail this item, worried teachers make it part of the curriculum and force-feed it with inappropriate drill and practice.

In the face of such items, teachers' only recourse is to resort to drill, drill, and more drill or minutiae and prematurely abstract symbolism.

State departments of education should take an active role in educating adminis-trators at all levels, boards of education, the media, teachers, and parents about how to teach math to young children, and how to assess it meaningfully.

Unfortunate outcomes

The result of this entire situation is to wreak havoc with the integrity of teachers and the reform efforts of state department consultants. The pervasive power of achievement tests, their narrow focuses, and the types of items with which they are comprised combine to produce a host of unintended, but nevertheless destructive, outcomes.

The Mathematics Report Card (Dossey, Mullis, Lindquist, & Chambers, 1988), which summarizes the results of the fourth national assessment of mathematics achievement, discusses the effects of the test-driven curriculum on children:

> The mathematical performance of students at ages 9, 13, and 17 has improved somewhat over the past eight years, yet a closer look at levels of proficiency indicates that most of the progress has occurred in the domain of lower-order skills. (p. 49)

> Evidence concerning the nature of mathematics education suggests that the curriculum continues to be dominated by paper-and-pencil drills on basic computation. Little evidence appears of any widespread use of calculators, computers, or mathematics projects. This picture reflects classrooms more concerned with students' rote use of procedures than with their understanding of concepts and development of higher-order thinking skills. The continuance of such a pattern offers little hope that the mathematics education of our children will achieve the goals being set by the recent educational excellence movement. (p. 12)

*   *   *

To summarize, standardized achievement testing has served to:

- perpetuate narrowly focused instruction with a preponderance of one right answer drill and practice;
- foster a more formal and abstract approach to basic skills than is developmentally appropriate for many children;
- accelerate curriculum downward as more and more teachers try to prepare more and more students for items less and less appropriate for a particular grade level;
- be a distinct and powerful disincentive for making curricular improvement since few (at any level) can risk a drop in test scores; and
- narrow the entire program to teaching first those skills covered by the test, often to the exclusion of other, perhaps more important, skills.

Directions for the future

The only way out of this dilemma requires that educators lead a frontal assault on the use of standardized tests and demand the responsible development of alternative and less destructive forms of assessment. *The Curriculum and Evaluation Standards for School Mathematics* (National Council of Teachers of Mathematics, 1989) tackles this point directly:

> The vision of mathematics education in the *Standards* places new demands on instruction and forces us to reassess the manner and methods by which we chart our students' progress. In an instructional environment that demands a deeper understanding of mathematics, testing instruments that call for only the identification of single correct responses no longer suffice. (p. 192)

Accordingly, to avoid the negative consequences outlined above, while meeting our legitimate needs for accountability, assessment, and alignment, it is imperative that we:

- eliminate entirely the use of these instruments prior to fourth grade, at which time their abstract, pencil-and-paper focus first becomes justifiable;

- educate teachers and administrators about how to provide developmentally appropriate math experiences in kindergarten and the primary grades;

- begin immediately to develop and institute programs of assessment that reflect current knowledge of appropriate curriculum and effective instruction; and

- institute widespread educational campaigns to better inform teachers, administrators, parents, school board members, and state level policymakers about the issues surrounding the use of these tests.

State departments of education should not mindlessly follow the mandates of legislatures and/or state boards of education. When educators in state departments become "yes" people who merely follow the wishes of officials insufficiently familiar with teaching and learning, children are the losers. State department people, too, must be accountable and justify their actions. "We are only following orders"never been an acceptable reason for actions in America.

Most state departments conduct in-service teacher education; we must do the same kind of work to enlighten local administrators and school boards. In mathematics, state departments can coordinate their efforts with those of the National Council of Teachers of Mathematics, which is working to translate the new standards into concrete actions.

Until and unless we make the changes outlined above, children will continue to be innocent pawns, who can only lose in the standardized testing games that grown-ups play with the best of intentions and worst of consequences.

Chapter 9

The Approach of a State Department

Deborah Murphy and Otis Baker

In light of the accountability pressures on practicing educators described in previous chapters, state policymakers also have the obligation to be accountable — to justify their decisions and to ensure that evaluation promotes explicit and well-conceptualized goals of education. Accountability begins with defining goals on the basis of the most valid scientific theory available. This chapter describes the beginning steps one state took to develop a system of accountability that makes sense for children, teachers, parents, and administrators.

In 1987, the Missouri Commissioner of Education created the Early Childhood Curriculum Task Force and charged it with developing a coherent curriculum/assessment framework for teachers and parents of children ages 3 through first grade. Although the 15-member task force includes some administrators, professors, and state department staff such as the Director of Early Childhood Education, it was decided that the majority would be teachers because

(a) they are most affected by curriculum/assessment decisions,

(b) they have the most direct experience with children and know the realities of classroom possibilities, and

(c) they are the legitimate agents of lasting change.

The Missouri Department of Elementary and Secondary Education decided from the beginning to offer the curriculum/assessment framework as an instructional tool for teachers and others to use on a voluntary basis. The initiative, which was later named Project CONSTRUCT, required no legislative or board approval because no one was forced to participate. Change was to be introduced through consultation and voluntary collaboration — the only way lasting change can be achieved.

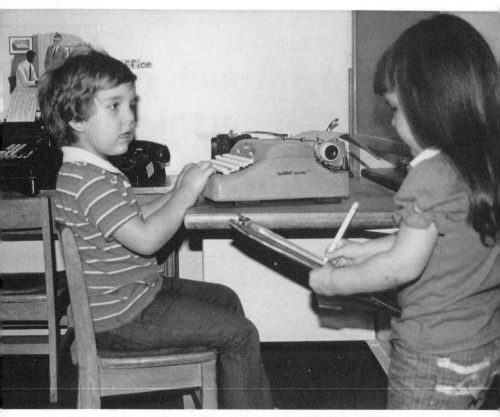

The Missouri Commissioner of Education created the Early Childhood Curriculum Task Force and charged it with developing a coherent curriculum/assessment framework for teachers and parents of children ages 3 through first grade. The majority of members were teachers because teachers are most affected by curriculum/ assessment decisions, they have the most direct experience with children and know the realities of classroom possibilities, and they are the legitimate agents of lasting change.

Accountability for what?

As stated in Chapter 2, the most important part of assessment begins with the definition of goals. If we want to assess children's progress, we must first make sure that the goals toward which children are progressing are valid in light of scientific research and theory. The task force, therefore, spent the first six months studying and trying to conceptualize goals. Although we were in agreement about general principles, we were not clearly in agreement about how to define goals. The criteria used for judging the worthiness of a goal changed as our knowledge expanded and deepened through reading and reflection and through discussions within our group and with other colleagues. We began to challenge commonly accepted notions of what should be included in a curriculum for young children, such as knowing names of colors, and to search for deeper and more general guideposts.

We adapted Kohlberg and Mayer's (1972) classification of approaches to the definition of goals and considered the following five: "bag of virtues," "prediction of success," "normal expectations," "consensus," and "theory/research." The first four approaches were not accepted. The rationale for rejecting them may provide insight to others interested in launching a new system.

Bag of virtues. This approach identifies positive traits "we" value in adults and transposes them onto children. While popular, this method has several flaws. It provides little direction when the traits we desire conflict. Consider two traits often valued by early childhood educators: sharing and standing up for one's rights. It is difficult to value both in a given situation (when children are fighting over a toy, for example). Also, a child's independence may be viewed by someone else as stubbornness. Defining goals with a list of virtues results in arbitrary, vague, numerous, and often conflicting goals (DeVries & Kohlberg, 1987).

Prediction of success. This approach emphasizes what children need to know to be successful at the next level of schooling. While everyone agrees that continuity is important, this method alone does not assure that the goals and objectives of the next level of schooling are sound. It also devalues the present stage of development. Being a kindergartner has value in and of itself. If this "readiness" approach were extended to its logical conclusion, those reading this sentence might be viewed as simply preparing for retirement.

Normal expectations. Educators and policymakers using this approach begin by asking, "What does a typical 3-year-old or 6-year-old do?"However, the simple act of tallying behavior does not bestow any special value on that behavior. As Lilian Katz (1986) has pointed out, there are many things that young children can do: babysit their younger siblings, watch bad television, and fill out reams of worksheets. The fact that children can do something does not necessarily mean that they should do it.

Consensus. Gaining consensus as a means of identifying goals has the advantage of broad ownership. Current educational administration principles often advocate techniques such as participatory management. Consenus is also consistent with democratic principles. However, unbridled consensus can have negative consequences. Slavery flourished and Hitler ruled by popular support. Consensus must be tempered with justice, equity, and knowledge. Agreement that the world is flat or that little children think like adults is nothing more than shared ignorance.

Theory/research. This was the approach we chose. It rests on informed decision making, that is, using the most accurate, complete, and consistent body of knowledge about young children and their development. A theoretical framework is the glue, or explanation, that holds scientific evidence together and enables us to avoid inconsistency and fragmentation. Like the blind man touching the elephant, without a theory, we cannot construct a sufficiently complete picture to know what (or, in the case of early education, whom) we are touching. If early education is ever to rise above sentiment or vague generalities, we must formulate and justify our goals and actions on the basis of sound scientific theory.

After deciding to conceptualize goals on the basis of a scientific theory and to use consensus to complete the picture, the task force examined various theories to identify the most complete and adequate explanation of young children's acquisition of knowledge. We came to the conclusion that constructivism best met these criteria. Since constructivism is explained in Chapter 2 in comparison with other scientific theories of learning such as behaviorism and associationism, we will not repeat that discussion here.

The task force's next job was to critically examine Piaget's (1948/ 1973) suggestion that autonomy should be the aim of education. We also examined the hierarchical conceptualization of goals described by Kamii and Kamii in Chapter 2. By the spring of 1988, we were in agreement that autonomy was the most desirable long-term goal of education because (a) a democratic society must educate its future citizens to become independent thinkers rather than obedient followers and (b) a pluralistic society cannot prescribe all the virtues every individual must have. An individual's independent, critical thinking about relevant factors naturally leads to autonomy, and while autonomy does not specify whether a person will have the qualities of a president of the United States, an artist, or anything else, it does ensure that the individual will think deeply about the decisions he or she will make. By definition, autonomy includes thoughtfulness, independent thinking, and high standards of morality (Piaget, 1932/1965).

The task force also agreed with the hierarchical conceptualization of goals because social interactions are important for moral and intellectual development and because the social atmosphere of a classroom greatly influences the possibility of moral and intellectual development. Children who are free to speak their minds and to do their own thinking develop more than those who are made to give "right" answers and to behave in the "right" way.

The task force then conceptualized more specific goals. We wrote countless drafts, which were revised during and after numerous long meetings and reviewed by over 800 people. Examples of topics we especially debated at length were the place of spoken and written language in the hierarchical conceptualization and how to deal with aesthetic and motor development.

During the 1988–89 school year, we identified 10 pilot sites representing public schools and child care programs throughout the state to

(a) test the possibility of implementing a constructivist framework,

(b) provide visitation sites for others interested in pursuing a constructivist approach,

(c) create a group of regional consultants from the sites who can speak firsthand about the curriculum and its possibilities, and

(d) offer information and guidance about ways to document children's development.

The 18 regional consultants from the pilot sites joined the task force and national leaders in debating curriculum goals. The results were unprecedented intellectual growth and commitment to the new framework on the part of hundreds of educators.

In the spring of 1989, we mailed more than 3,000 copies of the final draft of goals to all Missouri school districts, child care centers, and early childhood teacher educators, and other interested people for the purpose of soliciting their opinions and suggestions. We worked hard from the very beginning to inform and involve early childhood educators throughout the state so that Project CONSTRUCT would have broad ownership through honest, open discusssion and debate. The draft included an explanation of the importance of each goal, the definition of terms, and examples of how teachers can tell that a child has progressed toward each goal. We also sent these materials to the national consultants who had been involved all along in the many previous revisions. The circle of interest widened as more people became aware of the project and asked to become involved. Approximately 300 people are currently working with Project CONSTRUCT in some way.

In short, the Missouri Department of Elementary and Secondary Education has invested heavily in developing leaders who are highly educated teachers and administrators. The regional consultants from the pilot sites met monthly for a day with department staff for in-service education, mutual consultation, and networking. The regional consultants also participated in two week-long seminars to study constructivist education with national consultants. At other workshops and conferences, teachers and administrators refined their understanding of child development, "whole language," and a positive sociomoral environment. We provided a small library of professional books on constructivist education for each site at the beginning of the project, and collected and sent articles to the pilot sites every four to six weeks.

The department incurred all the expenses of developing these leaders. The exception was the cost of hiring substitute teachers when teachers attended meetings. Substitute teachers were paid by local districts, which had agreed to participate in the statewide effort to rethink the fundamentals of early childhood education.

Accountability by what means?

Methods of assessment cannot be developed before goals are clearly defined. Since we are not finished with the conceptualization and definition of goals, it is premature to discuss specific techniques. We can say, however, that half a dozen members of the Center for Educa-

We worked hard from the very beginning to inform and involve early childhood educators throughout the state so that Project CONSTRUCT would have broad ownership through honest, open discussion and debate. The draft included an explanation of the importance of each goal, the definition of terms, and examples of how teachers can tell that a child has progressed toward each goal. We also sent these materials to the national consultants who had been involved all along in the many previous revisions. The circle of interest widened as more people became aware of the project and asked to become involved.

tional Assessment of the University of Missouri in Columbia have been working all along in close collaboraton with department staff, task force members, pilot site participants including regional consultants, and other teachers to conceptualize goals, possible indicators, and examples, and to test some instruments.

Some basic decisions about our approach to assessment have been made. They are similar to those found in Chapters 2, 11, and 13 of this volume:

1. Teachers have to do the assessment if it is to be useful for teaching.
2. Assessment has to be rooted in classroom activities as much as possible.
3. Assessment has to take into account the process of development over time.

The reader must have noted two major differences between our approach to assessment and that of achievement testing.

First, putting teachers in charge is the opposite of excluding them from the evaluation process in the name of "objectivity."

Second, assessment must take into account each child's progress over time rather than comparing each child with other children on one particular day.

These are major differences that require pioneer work not only in assessment but also in teacher evaluation, the in-service education of administrators and teachers, and teacher certification. These accompanying changes are briefly discussed below.

Teacher evaluation. The way teachers are evaluated greatly influences how they behave in the classroom. The Missouri Excellence in Education Act of 1985 requires public school teachers to be evaluated with performance-based criteria, but the current generic state criteria do not adequately reflect the qualities desirable in early childhood education. Teacher evaluation also needs to be broadened to include an assessment of the environment the teacher creates. It is critical that the classroom be an environment that promotes children's development, rather than limiting it. Knowing that goals, teacher behaviors, attitudes, belief systems, and the environment must be aligned, we are engaged in developing better tools for teacher evaluation.

In-service/staff development. A strong network and support system needs to be in place to assist teachers, administrators, and parents who want to implement the constructivist framework. A state in-service plan is under way and will be implemented in 1990, when the assessment tools become available for dissemination.

Teacher certification. As early childhood education becomes more specialized, with different programs, funding sources, and regulations, in addition to the problem of continuity with the primary grades, teachers are finding it increasingly difficult to talk to one another about children. There needs to be a common core of knowledge, skills, and attitudes so that professionals can talk to each other and to parents in ways that do not conflict. Educators in special education must be as knowledgeable about child development, theory, and appropriate developmental practices as regular teachers. The department staff and other adminstrators and teachers in Missouri are working to define the competencies required of all professional educators who work with children from birth through age 8 or their families.

In conclusion

We often forget in the quick-fix mentality of today that the most important goals of education are to contribute to children's intellectual, social, and moral development in the long run. The story of the tortoise and the hare has never had much appeal in America, but we must remember that the tortoise won the race. As Eleanor Duckworth (1987) has wisely suggested, the important thing is not how *fast* we go but, how *far* we go.

Just as children have to construct their own knowledge and moral values from within, teachers and administrators, too, must develop from within if they are to institute lasting change. Any attempt to issue mandates and to police practitioners often results in surface compliance or "games." The construction of new ways of thinking scientifically takes time, but when it happens, educators cannot go back to the old ways of thinking. The leaders trained through the initiative of the Missouri state department are vocal and insistent about doing what is truly good for young children in the long run.

State departments of education, as well as teachers and local administrators, consciously or unconsciously choose to be perpetuators of the status quo, pawns of political power, or leaders in education. The question is: Do we have the will and the wisdom to pursue more enlightened ways of educating our young children — the adults of the 21st Century?

Chapter 10

Negative Effects of Achievement Testing in Literacy Development

Susan Harman*

I t's 9:30 in an average first grade classroom. The teacher has told the "morning story" (that is, the date and weather) and taken attendance, and the principal has made the announcements over the loudspeaker. Since the children are alive and alert, it's time for reading, the day's most important subject.

But "reading" in many a traditional first grade does not mean what we adults mean by reading; that is, snuggling into a comfortable armchair with a good book, or sitting at our desk with a challenging article. Instead, it means drawing lines from the picture of the ball to the letter *B*, finding the word *sat* in a list of three *sit*s and a *sat,* circling the words with the sound of *E* as in *egg,* filling in the missing final consonants, dividing words into syllables, and "bubbling in" answers to the five "comprehension" questions taken from a six-line "story."

Occasionally, a child will have an opportunity to read aloud a few sentences from her basal reader, in turn with six or seven other members of the reading group. Since this method of teaching requires accuracy in decoding, this child will be frequently interrupted by the teacher ("Don't just guess; think. What sound does *R* make?") or by other children's waving hands when she hesitates over a word. She will be preempted and corrected before she can call up her prior knowledge of the subject, use the context and syntax of the sentence as cues to the word, or hazard an intelligent guess. A justification for grouping children, rather than the teacher simply reading with one child at a time, is that the children who are not reading aloud can check their own competence by silently reading along. However, most are too anxious, or too bored, to take advantage of the safety of silence.

---

* My years of association with Deborah Meier—both in schools and out—inform everything I write, and particularly this chapter.

As for "writing," it consists of tracing over letters in workbooks, or filling a line with progressively inaccurate copies of some arbitrarily chosen letter. Even this dull exercise could be made more meaningful by giving each child her initial to practice, but Sarah is told "We're not up to *S* in the workbook yet."

When the children's morning enthusiasm has been deadened by "drill and kill" (Smith, 1986), and they are restless and tired, they are permitted to draw, build with blocks, or sometimes look at storybooks.

The vicious circle

It is no accident that this description of the morning "reading" lesson sounds more like taking a test than reading. As doing well on tests is substituted for knowing how to read, *authentic* reading and writing of *authentic* texts (Edelsky & Smith, 1984; Edelsky & Draper, in press) has been replaced by test-like activities. In fact, it is not so much that practicing for the tests is stealing time away from authentic literacy activities, but rather that, in many classrooms, school itself has become a test-like activity.

The determination of curriculum by tests is variously described as "teaching to the tests," "test-driven curriculum," or, most recently, "curriculum alignment." This last term is perhaps the most revealing, since it clearly implies that the tests come first. That is, the tests are the given, and it is the curriculum that must be brought into conformance with them.

The typical morning described above may vary from community to community in some details. But it won't vary much. As the recent *Report Card on Basal Readers* (Goodman, Shannon, Freeman, & Murphy, 1988) points out, there is a vicious and hermetic spiral that starts from the test, goes directly to the design of the basal readers, to their accompanying workbooks, to their unit tests, and back to the standardized tests. Since 94% of teachers use basal readers every day, one can predict from

Photo p. 113: *Doing well on "reading" tests has been substituted for knowing how to read, reading, and enjoying reading. Therefore, "reading" time in classrooms no longer includes the good children's literature and experience/writing-about-it/reading-it approach prevalent before the 1960s. "Reading time" in most schools has come to mean test-like decoding activities using basal readers or worksheets. We need to get back to reading good books.*

the content of the tests a community uses what kind of basal series that community bought and what any morning's reading activities will be.

Power of the tests

Test results by school are published in the *New York Times* and in local papers in other communities. As has been stated elsewhere in this book, children's scores often determine whether they are held back, promoted, or sent to classes for the gifted or disabled; class scores affect the evaluation and merit pay of teachers; and a school's reputation as "good" or "bad" rests on its scores. It is clear that the tests wield immense power.

Another index of their power is their costs. It is extremely difficult to get accurate data on the costs of testing; even estimates are hard to arrive at. The best figure I could tease out of the New York City Board of Education's budget is $6 million per year, and that leaves out many indirect costs that would swell this figure by several times. If we divided this number by our million schoolchildren, we could buy each child a couple of paperback classics, or a set of magic markers and a journal in which he could write his observations of the hatching butterflies, his oral history interviews with his grandparents, or his imagined voyage into the future. If we added in the cost of basals and their accompanying paraphernalia (workbooks, worksheets, unit tests, teachers' manuals, wall charts), estimated at $300 million per year nationally, we could probably put a word processor in every classroom.

The tests' power derives primarily from the ostensible objectivity and scientific appearance of their numbers. Although all test manuals urge caution in interpreting scores, it is only the grade level or percentile that anyone in fact pays attention to. Everyone knows those numbers are the product of careful and expensive research, and everyone thinks that, unlike teachers' evaluations, they must be objective. This illusion of objectivity is so powerful that it cows otherwise confident and competent teachers into doubting their own observations and judgments, and deferring to the test scores.

Standardized, norm-referenced tests are not like drivers' tests, which are constructed so that each of us can do well on them. The achievement tests given in school are made so that half the children will score below "grade level." Therefore, tests cannot simply evaluate what children have learned because then everyone might do well. Some questions must be hard enough—or obscure enough—to guarantee that only a few children will get them right. That is, they must tap what has *not* been learned. So then schools must begin teaching to those questions, and the vicious spiral of alignment, premature teaching, and drilling whirls on.

Teachers are distracted from considering individual children's interests, talents, or needs; in fact, such essential concerns become counterproductive in a test-aligned curriculum. The curriculum has been prescribed, page by page and exercise by exercise, by experts. And it "works"—the better children do on the basal unit tests, the better they do on the standardized tests. This is not surprising because they are, after all, the same, "aligned" test.

Some teachers bring storybooks, stationery, calligraphy pens, comics, magic markers, and blank bound books into their classrooms. There is growing interest in print-rich classroom environments, and there is a corresponding avalanche of publications on how and why to teach this way (Newman, 1985; Kontos, 1986; Schickedanz, 1986; Teale & Martinez, 1988; Throne, 1988; Weaver, 1988; Strickland & Morrow, 1989). But most teachers think that constructing an open-ended curriculum that is responsive to different children's interests and needs takes time away from "covering the material" prescribed by the tests. In fact, the test-like "reading" and "writing" activities take up so much classroom time that teachers rarely have an opportunity to simply observe children reading and writing.

Effects on less advantaged children

Children who have been read to at home—who have probably already learned to read by the "lap method" before coming to school—know what reading is. These children may see the exercises as an opportunity to show off, as an indifferent way of passing time, or as just boring. But there are other children who have not been read to, who do not already have a working definition of what reading is, or who have for some reason become stuck in the process of acquiring literacy. These other children may be confused by the exercises and may lose confidence in their capacity to read and write.

The powerful myth of the tests' objectivity has serious implications for the children who do not score well and who are beginning, shaky, or problematic readers. Many teachers and administrators rely on the test scores as *true* and consign the low scorers to the "Turtles" reading group, where they get a very different education from the "Eagles." As studies of reading groups have documented, the lowest group gets more busy work, is interrupted more, reads only one-third as many words as the highest group, and has a permanent membership (Rist, 1973; McDermott & Aron, 1978; Allington, 1983). Once a "Turtle," always a "Turtle."

As these children read less and less and get further and further behind the others, they are often moved from the lowest reading group to a Resource Room. There they are told to connect the picture of a baby bunny to the picture of its mother by drawing a *very* straight line, or to clap their hands to match the Morse Code-like pattern of dots in a workbook (or to make dots to match clapping hands). This "perceptual-motor training" persists, despite there being not a shred of evidence that it improves children's reading, or that it has any connection to reading at all (Coles, 1987). Finally, in desperation, these children are sent, for at least part of the day, to self-contained special

The "whole language" approach to reading quality children's literature, and writing and guess-spelling about a wide variety of intriguing real experiences, with emphasis on meaning rather than on skills, is coming back because new research and theory strongly indicate that it is by far the best way to educate children effectively.

education classrooms, where they continue connecting bunnies. (In New York City, for instance, the rate of decertification back to regular education is only 5%.) In these forgotten classes children read—to say nothing of painting, engaging in social studies or science, playing music, or writing—scarcely at all. Special education teachers are trained in a strongly behaviorist tradition and concentrate on skills. In this skills approach to teaching, painting, social studies, science, and music are considered to be frills.

Since reading is making meaning out of print, rather than mere decoding, as Kamii and Kamii explain in Chapter 2, the more you know about the world, the more meaningful anything you read is, and the better reader you are. Conversely, the less you know about the world, the harder it is to make sense of what you read. Every minute of children's time squandered on test-like exercises is a minute *not* invested in finding out about the world. The price children pay is a double one: They know less about the world, and they read less well.

The future

There is growing agreement among researchers, teachers, and teacher educators about how best to help children acquire literacy. We know from the literature on language acquisition that babies learn to talk without a single lesson. The ideal conditions for learning to talk are a risk-free setting in which proficient speakers respond to the learner's approximations of adult speech. Frank Smith (1973, 1975, 1983, 1985, 1986, 1988), among others, has spent the last 20 years documenting the effectiveness of the same conditions for learning to read. He recommends a safe, comfortable setting in which a child sits with both a book that is well-crafted and a proficient reader who can help when the child feels a need for it.

Basal readers are carefully crafted but written with wrong assumptions about what is hard or easy for a child to read. Their authors assume that short, bland, frequently occurring words (such as *go, will, to, she,* and *the*) are easier than long, unusual words (such as *ghost, naughty, pickle,* and *brontosaurus*). In fact, however, the basal words are phonically irregular (*the* does not rhyme with *she; go* does not rhyme with *to*), they look similar, and they are often abstract (try drawing a picture of *will*). Furthermore, many of their "plots" are hardly intriguing or exciting.

Well-crafted stories, on the other hand, tell a real story using real syntax and juicy words, so a child can apply her prior knowledge of language and the world and make sense of the text. The child evaluates herself in *real* reading: If what she reads does not make sense, she knows she is not reading well. On the rare occasions when she cannot make sense of the print, there is a person (a parent, an older child, or a teacher) who simply tells her the word. Children who are motivated and curious about print make connections between the letters they see and the word they hear *in context.*

More recently, Lucy Calkins (1986), among others, has augmented Smith's work with hers on writing. In this approach to writing, children begin to think of themselves as authors by choosing their own topics, composing narratives they care about, inventing their own spelling, editing and revising their drafts, understanding the function of punctuation and spelling in context, and, in a word, behaving like real writers. Here again, evaluation of their work is built into the process of conferring about and revising their own writing.

In fact, the burgeoning pedagogical movement known as "whole language" (Goodman, 1986) is rapidly accumulating evidence that children acquire literacy in the same natural ways they acquire spoken language. Children learn to read by reading, rather than by doing test-like exercises. They also learn to write by writing, rather than by filling in worksheets. The ideal early childhood classroom is one that is full of written language in books, magazines, comics, recipes, directions, labels, signs, lists, and notes—a classroom in which children are free to explore and experiment with talking, reading, and writing (Bredekamp, 1987). A good environment for developing literacy is one in which children get a great deal of feedback that is useful and meaningful *to them,* rather than one in which they are drilled in the mechanics of decoding isolated words.

Better ways of teaching literacy *are* known. New approaches to assessment are also known, as can be seen in the following chapter. However, achievement tests are preventing this new knowledge from being more widely used in classrooms.

It is time for grown-ups to stop playing the vote-getting game and the looking-good game. Educators must think more seriously about our long-term goals for children and stop the drill and practice that have improved test scores but have sacrificed children's creativity, self-confidence, and enjoyment of reading. As Engel suggests in the next chapter, we can and must move from calibrating children's achievements to celebrating them.

Chapter 11

An Approach to Assessment in Early Literacy

Brenda S. Engel

According to the common wisdom, children learn to read when they get to school, except those few, like John Stuart Mill, whose parents teach them at home at age 2 or 3, or like Heidi, who simply teach themselves. Progressive educators, however, have long understood reading and writing as developmental, beginning virtually at birth. Over the past two decades, a body of international research has reinforced this view of literacy learning. (See work by Smith, 1971; Clay, 1979; Holdaway, 1979; Ferreiro & Teberosky, 1982; Graves, 1982; Harste, Woodward, & Burke, 1984; and Goodman, 1986, among others.) Reading and writing, along with speaking and listening, are understood as facets of language learning, and reading itself is increasingly understood as the ability to get meaning from print (rather than the ability to decode print into sound). This new conception necessitates new approaches to assessment.

It is not an exaggeration to say that acquisition of language, that uniquely human and almost magical capability, begins at birth with the infant's response to voice. By the time children get to school, whether to preschool or kindergarten, they already know an uncanny amount about oral and written language: They can speak and understand complex sentences and know that print usually represents words; they can probably read some words (like "STOP" or "Corn Chex") and write a few letters (like X and O); they may also know about beginnings and endings (like "Once upon a time . . . " and "The End").

Most middle-class children know that newspapers and fairy tales differ in tone; that menus, phone books, and shopping lists are not composed of sentences; that puns are funny; and that, no matter how hard they try, they won't be able to teach a dog to talk. Children from less privileged backgrounds, too, have acquired a good deal of this kind of knowledge before school.

Given a reasonably positive school situation, children will go right on learning about language. Sometime in the early elementary grades, most become able to get meaning from unfamiliar texts without help. Most also learn to write conventionally enough so that others can read their compositions. My point is that, under favorable conditions, literacy, as an aspect of language learning, develops from birth on in an ever-expanding, uninterrupted continuum; it is driven by the child's own impulse toward competence and participation in the world's events.

Keeping track is one way to evaluate progress

Evaluation as "keeping track" begins at birth and continues into the school years. Parents and caretakers are likely to note a baby's first words: "baa" (for "bottle") or "gaga" (for "doggie"), sometimes even recording such milestones in a baby book. They might note when an infant first tries to put together two words or, later on, might save a child's simulation of a shopping list or crude attempt to form the letters in her own name.

"Keeping track" in this manner constitutes a kind of evaluation. Because ordinary development is both expected and celebrated, the overall tone is positive and confirming. There is always, of course, a slight possibility that ordinary development won't occur—that something may be wrong—so early home-style evaluation acts as reassurance of expected progress.

There are several reasons why "keeping track" seems a desirable way to approach evaluation of early literacy learning, at least through second grade:

- It meets the need for accountability while preserving the recognition and encouragement that have successfully supported growth and change before schooling.
- It is based on an assumption of success, not failure; is primarily descriptive rather than judgmental; and is not norm referenced.
- It provides an account of what happens, when, and how, rather than what should happen.

When parents keep track of infants' learning, they themselves are the monitors, not responsible to anyone beyond possibly a grandparent or two. The moment a child enters school, however, the responsibility for keeping track shifts: Virtually everyone has a vested interest in school-children's learning, from the children and their families to teachers, administrators, school board members, and the larger community of taxpayers.

The problem becomes, then, how to provide adequate information to each of these constituencies, but preserve the usefulness and positive quality of the before-school kind of evaluation. The problem is complicated by the fact that different constituencies need different kinds of information in different forms: Children need to know that they're making progress and that their abilities and special qualities are appreciated; parents (or caretakers) need more specific information and reassurance about children's progress; teachers need information on how and what children are learning to use as feedback for teaching; administrators and community members need to know, in summary form, the progress children are making.

A possible solution to the problem of the different needs of various constituencies is to organize evaluation information on three levels:

1. raw descriptive data about individual children,
2. summaries and interpretations of the raw data about individual children, and
3. quantified information about groups.

On the following pages, I suggest some possible contents for these three levels without attempting to provide recipes or comprehensive programs for assessment.

Level One: Primary data

This collection of data—literacy interviews, reading tapes, and teacher observations—should meet the needs of teachers and children and, to some extent, parents.

Literacy folders

Collections of children's work are the principal means of keeping track: individual folders containing periodic, dated samples of drawings, other artwork, and writing (including ideas; plans; lists of books, stories, and poems read). The contents of the folders should be systematic, up-to-date, and available for review by teachers, children, and, during conferences, parents. Samples of children's uncorrected writing

Keeping track of children's development and learning in writing and reading by periodically collecting their work in literacy folders, making oral reading tapes at intervals, and observing one child throughout a day and taking notes to be added to the folder are all aspects of "Level One" evaluation. These data should meet the needs of teachers, children, and, to some extent, parents. Progress is obvious, more tangible than complex scores and statistics.

(that is, with the original "invented spelling") on child-selected subjects are of particular interest. The samples convey the history and quality of a child's involvement in literacy learning.

The most important advantage of this kind of evidence is its undoubted authenticity. The children's work stands for itself, proves its own point. Learning, rather than being claimed or expressed in percentiles or grade levels, is made visible. Direct evidence is both interesting and significant because it conveys quality, the element that is lost as information is abstracted, quantified, and prepared for a wider audience. Actual examples retain the recognizable idiosyncratic character of the particular child as well as the characteristics the child has in common with all other children.

Literacy interviews

I have used audiotape recordings to keep track of children's progress into literacy from preschool into the primary grades. For preschoolers or children who are "emergent readers," the taping sessions take the form of "literacy interviews." I ask the child to choose a favorite book. We then settle down together in a relatively secluded corner of the classroom to "read" the book. I turn on the tape recorder and begin with some questions:

> "Can you tell me where the front of the book is? " "What is this book about? " "Can you put your finger on where the story begins? "

I encourage the child to tell me the story as we turn the pages, or, if it seems indicated, I read the story aloud, stopping frequently so the child can guess at a word or anticipate what is about to happen. We look at the pictures as well as the print.

The occasion is meant to be relaxed and friendly. I do, however, have an agenda: to assess where the child is on the developmental continuum in respect to reading and what his or her feelings are about books. Specifically, I'm curious about whether the child likes the book, has a sense of story and can paraphrase the text, "gets the point," understands directionality (left-right, up-down), knows the significance of any punctuation marks, recognizes any letters or words, and understands the relationship of lower and upper case letters. I ask the child also about other favorite books, whether there are books available at home, whether she is read to at home and how often, and how much television she watches.

The interview is relatively short — about 10 minutes — and I make a few descriptive notes as well as recording the session. I label the tape (preferably the 60-minute kind) with the child's name and the date of the interview. The next interview or oral reading, also dated, is put on the same tape, beginning where the previous one left off. The inventory (described in Level Two) can be used to record information from the interview in a more formal way. (If the teacher conducts interviews in the classroom, she may have to do them in bits and pieces; tape recording may not be possible at all and the teacher's notes will then constitute the record.)

Oral reading tapes

Children who are beginning to read on their own can be recorded reading a story at an appropriate level of difficulty (i.e., not too hard and not too easy). Show the child a selection of stories, reading the titles and giving some idea of what each story is about. The child then selects an appropriate one to read aloud into the tape recorder. (Most second graders and some first graders can, with clear instructions, record themselves.) Afterward, ask the child, "Can you tell me what the story was about?" ("retelling").

Oral reading tapes provide excellent records of children's development in reading. A teacher or parent will find it more informative and interesting to listen to a tape of a child reading a story than to review reading scores. Children themselves are endlessly interested in their own work and recorded history, particularly as they are reminded of their younger selves and see evidence of growth and change.

Although the collection of tapes for a whole class will be useful to mark the progress of individuals and the group, some can be selectively scored—not necessarily for *all* children, but for those children for whom more detailed information might be useful. The method of scoring, shown in Table 11.1, is a modified version of miscue analysis (Goodman, 1979). It may, at first, seem complicated and time consuming. However, it soon becomes fairly automatic: A teacher experienced in the method can score a tape, using the Oral Reading Appraisal Form shown in Figure 11.1, in about 10 to 30 minutes, depending on the length of the text read.

Table 11.1
Procedures for Scoring Oral Reading Tapes*

1. *Marking text:* Use photocopy of text read.

- Listen to tape, underlining all mistakes (where spoken word differs from printed one). Optional: Write above printed word what reader actually said, when it differed from text. Don't count the same mistake twice.
- Indicate self-corrections by putting "C" above word corrected.
- Circle any words omitted.
- Put caret (∧) in space if extra word is added, writing in extra word above.
- If letters or words are reversed, mark with horizontal S (∽).
- Make notes on retelling (comprehension, completeness) and on particular qualities of reading (fluency, expressiveness, nature of mistakes, etc.).

* For use with Oral Reading Appraisal Form (Figure 11.2)

2. *Preparing to score reading:*

- Count and note total number of words in text.
- Go through text, putting slash (/) in margin opposite each mistake.
- Go through text a second time and put line through slashes (X) where mistakes have not been corrected (no "C" above word) or if it is not "supportive of meaning" (i.e., if it destroys syntax or meaning). For example, if the child reads, "It was a nice house" instead of "It was a nice home," the word "house" counts as a meaningful mistake and you don't cross out the slash. But if the child reads, "It was a nice harm," the mistake destroys meaning, and you should put a cross through the slash: X.

3. *Scoring:*

- Accuracy rate: total number of words minus number of mistakes plus self-corrections divided by the total number of words.

$$\frac{\text{words} - \text{mistakes} + \text{self-corrections}}{\text{total words}}$$

- Meaningful mistake rate: total number of single slashes divided by total number of single and crossed slashes.

$$\frac{\text{total} /}{\text{total} / + X}$$

- Self-correction rate: total number of self-corrections divided by total number of single and crossed slashes.

$$\frac{\text{total self-corrections}}{\text{total} / + X}$$

- Comprehension or retelling score:
  1 = fragmentary understanding
  2 = partial understanding
  3 = fairly complete understanding
  4 = full and complete understanding
- Text level: Use either publisher's text level equivalent or estimate level based on comparison with those of published texts. Levels do not represent grade levels; they are the publishers' arbitrary numbering of texts.

The accuracy score is important only as baseline information on the appropriateness of the text level. If literal word-by-word accuracy is below 95%, the child is likely to flounder and lose ability to use strategies he would ordinarily have at his disposal. If the accuracy rate is 100, the child could probably handle a more difficult text.

Both the meaningful mistake rate and the self-correction rate assess the child's determination to have the text make sense. In general, the higher the percentage, the more the child can be said to be reading for meaning. (If a child reads with near 100% accuracy, however, these percentages will have less significance, since there will be less opportunity for constructive mistakes or self-corrections.)

Figure 11.1
Oral Reading Appraisal Form

Student _____ Date of birth _____

Grade _____ Teacher _____ School _____

Date of reading _____ Favorite book read _____

Name of text read _____ Level of text _____

Accuracy rate:

$$\frac{\text{total words} - \text{total mistakes} + \text{total self-corrections}}{\text{total words}}$$

$$= \rule{4cm}{0.4pt}$$

Meaningful mistakes rate:

$$\frac{\text{meaningful mistakes}}{\text{total mistakes}}$$

$$= \rule{4cm}{0.4pt}$$

Self-correction rate:

$$\frac{\text{self-corrections}}{\text{total mistakes}}$$

$$= \rule{4cm}{0.4pt}$$

Comments:

Teacher observations

Teachers are the best sources of descriptive data on children. They know individual children well and are likely to be present at significant moments—moments of visible learning. Teachers too can use their observations to inform teaching. Note taking, however, can be difficult in a demanding classroom situation. A few suggestions may help:

- Focus on one child as much as possible for one day.
- Keep on hand a roll of gummed labels on which to write brief observational notes at moments during the day. At the end of the day, date labels and stick them on the inside cover of the child's folder.

- Make both language and content as descriptive as possible.
- Avoid making ambitious plans or setting schedules that will be hard to maintain; consistency is more important than frequency.

The following observation was made by a kindergarten teacher in an urban public school:

> When he was finished with his journal picture, he surprisd me by suddenly starting to write various letters on his page: P for Philip and then said E for Eliza (later also said Z for Eliza!), B for Binyamin. I had no idea that he knew all those letters, much less than he associated them correctly with names.

A continuous collection of primary data is, like the baby book, descriptive, affirming, and relevant, a rich mine of sequential material that embodies learning and can inform teaching. It is also unwieldy, however, and at some point it calls for review and interpretation—which brings me to the second level of evaluation.

Level Two: Summaries of individual children's progress

This second level of evaluation, still a way of "keeping track," interprets and summarizes the primary data. It includes teacher notes and comments, inventories, and analyses of oral reading tapes. No new information is added.

Teacher notes and comments

Teachers should review each child's literacy folder periodically, adding at this time to their own descriptive notes and making further comments on breakthroughs in understanding, interests, progress in mastering conventions, expressiveness, and so on. Such reviews can be in preparation for parents conferences, for year-end reports, or simply for routine record-keeping scheduled regularly throughout the school year.

The following example is excerpted from an anecdotal year-end report to parents of a kindergarten child.

> Of all the children in the class, P has probably made the most spectacular progress this year! One of the youngest, fully a year younger than the oldest child, P entered the class without separation

problems but appeared bewildered and withdrawn. He didn't know how to store the blocks by size, he couldn't count his crackers correctly, and he didn't speak.

By the late fall, P started to get more involved with materials in the classroom. He also became much more social and began to imitate some of the activities of the other children, particularly counting and sorting games. His oral language developed dramatically at this point. P's pattern seems to be to observe for a long time and take everything in quietly. Then, when he feels confident, he tries out a new activity for himself.

Figure 11.2
Descriptive Inventory

	yes	possibly	not yet
1. Enjoys books and stories			
2. Seeks book experiences, asks for or goes to books spontaneously			
3. Is curious about print			
4. Experiments with written language			
5. Is able to follow plot, sequences			
6. Can predict words, phrases			
7. Knows story comes from print			
8. Will tell story of familiar text, turning pages			
9. Knows directional conventions: left-right, top-bottom			
10. Understands print entities: words, letters			
11. Understands phonetic principle: letters related to speech sounds			
12. Understands consistency principle: same word is spelled the same way			
13. Knows 12 or more letter sounds			
14. Tries invented spelling			
15. Approximates reading with familiar text			
16. Recognizes 12 or more words			
17. Can sound out some words			
18. Knows two or more conventions of punctuation			

Literacy inventories

Inventories are summaries of children's literacy learning. Completed on the basis of the primary data, they are useful ways of "taking stock." An example is shown in Figure 11.2.

Inventories are not to be confused with check lists or scope-and-sequence charts. Unlike a check list, an inventory has meaning in terms of the overall picture: No single item represents a necessary achievement. Also, *unlike check lists and scope-and-sequence charts, which are set out ahead of the child pointing the way, inventories follow or "keep track of " what has already happened. This distinction is important: It concerns the difference between prescription and description. We are describing what is — in other words, "keeping track" — not prescribing what should be.* The procedures detailed in this chapter all depend on description and assume, as I stated at the beginning, that literacy learning for children is a natural extension of language development.

Oral reading tapes

The procedures involved in taping oral reading samples have already been outlined. The scoring procedures are shown in Table 11.1.

Level Three: Quantified information about groups

The third level of evaluation, which includes class summaries, statistics, and graphs, is designed for administrators and the public. With the exception of class summaries, this quantified information will hold less interest for teachers, children, and parents. The information, which should be assembled by administrative personnel (i.e., not by teachers), is abstracted from the primary data, some of it by way of the interpreted date in Level Two of evaluation. No new instruments or information are added except, perhaps, routine school and school department statistics.

Class summaries

Class summaries, in anecdotal form, are useful for school administrators (who can, in turn, further condense the information for central office records) in order to "flag" children who might be in need of

"Level Two" of this kind of evaluation interprets and summarizes the primary data that the teacher has collected. It includes teacher notes and comments, and inventories and analyses of oral reading tapes. No new data are added. "Level Three" is quantified information designed for administrators and the public. This information is assembled by administrators, not teachers (teachers have little use for most of it).

attention. Following is an example of such a summary of a first grade class (names have been changed):

> Twenty-nine children (in two classes) were recorded reading aloud: 18 boys and 11 girls. Six children, about a fifth of the class, were still "emergent readers," not able to make sense of an unfamiliar text: Kendall Arthur, Marian Jasper, Robert Merriam, Robert Aventino, Jonathan Tinbergen, and Katherine Rantulli. Katherine Rantulli had been retained from the previous year. This is about the expected proportion, roughly the same as in previous years. The average text level read with over 95% accuracy was level 6, up two levels from the previous year's first grade. (Levels do not represent grade levels but rather publishers' arbitrary numbering of texts.)
>
> The following seven students, although able to "decode" a text with fair word-by-word accuracy, were not able to retell the content with much detail: Colin Cameron, David Santiago, Donna Judson, Barbara Jordan, Hasan Said, Leo Albion, and Uri David.
>
> On the whole, children who had been in the school the previous year, in kindergarten, were reading on a slightly higher level and with better comprehension, more self-correction, and more demand for meaning. Word-by-word accuracy rates were about the same as that of the new children.

Statistics

Information about reading levels (from tape recordings) and results of literacy inventories can be summarized in numerical tables. An example is shown in Table 11.2. Writing, an equally important aspect of literacy learning, is, like other art forms, not easily amenable to quantitative representation. We have kept records of word and sentence counts but have not yet developed a very satisfactory way of summarizing quality.

Graphs

Reading levels can be effectively presented in graphic form. Figure 11.3 shows reading levels of 10 children grades 2 to 4. Kept over time, graphs like this one will effectively illustrate progress. A similar graph can be made with class averages over three (or more) years.

Table 11.2
Oral Reading Score of 10 Children for 1987 and 1988

Child	Oral Reading Score for 1987				
	Accuracy ratio (%)	Meaningful mistake ratio (%)	Self-correction ratio (%)	Comprehension estimate	Text level
1	97	50	33	4	2
2	96	29	10	3	3
3	*	*	*	*	*
4	90	21	18	2	2
5	94	33	15	3	4
6	92	53	25	3	4
7	96	50	26	4	5
8	95	38	10	4	2
9	99	50	30	2	2
10	98	71	40	4	3

Child	Oral Reading Score for 1988				
	Accuracy ratio (%)	Meaningful mistake ratio (%)	Self-correction ratio (%)	Comprehension estimate	Text level
1	*	*	*	*	*
2	96	59	27	2	6
3	93	50	27	4	4
4	97	64	30	4	8
5	96	77	22	3	10
6	95	63	10	3	7
7	95	80	13	3	8
8	95	85	42	4	5
9	98	36	45	3	7
10	98	100	50	4	8

Note: Text level is the publisher's rating. It does not denote a grade.
* = not tested

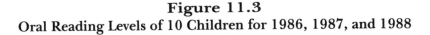

Figure 11.3
Oral Reading Levels of 10 Children for 1986, 1987, and 1988

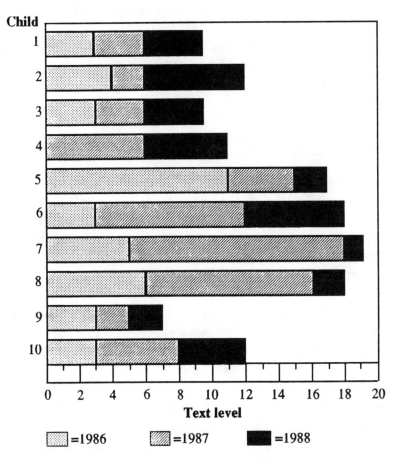

Feasibility

Because of differences among schools in resources, available personnel, teachers' schedules and responsibilities, and class sizes, it is possible here to make only modest suggestions for helping "keeping track" become classroom reality:

1. Enlist children's participation, particularly in collecting and dating work samples and tape-recording oral reading.
2. Build data collection into the instructional program, scheduling activities at regular intervals for the academic year.

3. Use any help you can get, from assistants, parents, student teachers, other available adults, or students from upper elementary classes.

4. Don't be too ambitious. Less on a regular basis is better than more inconsistently.

5. Central office personnel, not classroom teachers, should assemble Level Three, the quantified data, although teachers should be consulted to check for accuracy.

Principles of evaluation

The following principles, which are consistent with developmental theory, inform the procedures suggested in this chapter.

1. To be significant, evaluation of literacy learning should be concerned with real, not contrived, activities: real reading and writing rather than skills testing.

2. Description should be primary and provide the basis for interpretation and evaluation.

3. Evaluation of a developmental process like literacy learning should itself be developmental, that is, longitudinal.

4. The primary function of evaluation is to inform teaching.

5. Evaluation should be supportive of learning.

6. Evaluation should recognize the individual character of the learner — allowing differences in both styles and rates of learning.

Finally, evaluation that dampens children's natural desire to participate in the surrounding culture and that discriminates or labels cannot be justified in any terms: not in the name of policy setting or accountability. To see high standardized test scores as an educational goal is surely to live in an Alice-in-Wonderland world — where, ultimately, no one except politicians gets anywhere. The game may be making political vulnerable education *look good,* but we cannot allow it to be played when it results in making young children *feel bad.* The determining criterion of good literacy evaluation can be direct and sensible: whether both process and results bring each child greater access to the pleasures and benefits of reading and writing.

Chapter 12

Negative Effects of Achievement Testing in Mathematics

Constance Kamii and Mieko Kamii

Kathy is a bright second grader who loves worksheets and who feels competent and industrious as she solves problems. When she finishes a page, she is proud of herself and looks forward to seeing the Cs ("correct") that will decorate her answers. She will feel even more encouraged to continue working by the smiley face drawn by the teacher at the top of her page.

For Mike, however, worksheets are not a source of joy. For him, a problem like $7 + 8$ is easy, but one like $27 + 28$ is a dance of the digits. Though he does his work conscientiously, his sheets are invariably returned with patches of Cs and Xs. For Mike, mathematics has already become "doing what you're supposed to do, and then you wait to see how many you got right."

Worksheets are behavioristic instructional devices that do little to provoke any real thinking. Unfortunately, runaway testing has contributed to the greater use of worksheets and other instructional devices that reinforce the idea of "mathematics as a body of fixed facts and skills to be acquired, not as a tool for developing a particular kind of intellectual power in the student" (Goodlad, 1984, p. 209).

The National Research Council (1989), representing the work of the Mathematical Sciences Education Board, the Board on Mathematical Sciences, and their joint Committee on the Mathematical Sciences in the Year 2000, described the negative effects of achievement testing on mathematics instruction:

> Multiple-choice tests as used in America lead to widespread abuses, which the public rarely recognizes:
>
> • Tests become ends in themselves, not means to assess educational objectives. Knowing this, teachers often teach to the tests, not to the curriculum or to the children.

- Tests stress lower- rather than higher-order thinking, emphasizing student responses to test items rather than original thinking and expression.
- Test scores are sensitive to special coaching. . . .
- Timed tests stressing speed inhibit learning for many students. . . .
- Tests provide snapshots of performance under the most stressful environment for students rather than continuous information about performance in a supportive atmosphere.

Too often, good intentions in testing can lead to very bad results. Minimal competency testing often leads to minimal performance, where the floor becomes a ceiling. In stressing the importance of basic skills, such tests fail to encourage able students to progress as far as they can. . . .

To assess development of a student's mathematical power, a teacher needs to use a mixture of means: essays, homework, projects, short answers, quizzes, blackboard work, journals, oral interviews, and group projects. Only broad-based assessment can reflect fairly the important, higher-order objectives of mathematics curricula. (pp. 68–70)

Many teachers are already assessing children in the preceding ways. Achievement testing ignores and discourages these procedures and treats test scores as if they revealed the only "truth." The National Research Council goes on to conclude:

As we need standards for curricula, so we need standards for assessment. We must ensure that tests measure what is of value, not just what is easy to test. If we want students to investigate, explore, and discover, assessment must not measure just mimicry mathematics. By confusing means and ends, by making testing more important than learning, present practice holds today's students hostage to yesterday's mistakes. (p. 70)

The National Council of Teachers of Mathematics (1989) has also called for sweeping changes in instruction as well as in methods of evaluating the outcomes of K–12 mathematics. Recognizing that reform in mathematics education will not become a reality as long as standardized achievement tests are used as accountability measures, the NCTM proposed new standards for evaluation. Among the proposed standards are that:

- all aspects of mathematical knowledge and its connections be assessed [rather than a large number of isolated, lower level skills]; and

- instruction and curriculum be considered equally in judging the quality of a program [rather than considering only the number of correct answers on tests]. (pp. 190–191)

The National Assessment of Educational Progress (Dossey, Mullis, Lindquist, & Chambers, 1988) reported that the recent improvement in test scores has been due mostly to better performance in lower order skills (computation rather than problem solving). The reader is referred to Chapter 8 for the details of this report.

Worksheets are not very effective as instructional devices because they do little to provoke any real thinking. Paradoxically, runaway testing has contributed to the greater use of worksheets and other instructional devices that reinforce the idea of mathematics as a body of fixed facts and skills to be acquired, not as a tool for developing a particular kind of intellectual power in children.

There are better ways of teaching primary mathematics than relying on skill-and-drill worksheets. This chapter offers some examples and addresses the question of why achievement testing discourages the use of better teaching strategies, even by individuals who are by all other counts excellent teachers.

Goals and objectives

As explained in Chapter 2, different theories of learning and development lead to the conceptualization of different goals and objectives. Traditional math educators who do not distinguish between social knowledge and logico-mathematical knowledge (see Chapter 2) have as their objectives the giving of correct answers and the reading and writing of mathematical symbols, arguably the most superficial aspect of primary arithmetic. In kindergarten, traditionalists emphasize counting objects and writing numerals. First grade objectives typically include writing correct answers to problems such as $6 + 4 =$ _____, $10 - 3 =$ _____, and $6 +$ _____ $= 10$; learning the symbols for "equality," "greater than," and "less than"; and using the conventional form to represent statements such as "there are ten birds and four fly away." Second graders are expected to learn rules for double-column addition and subtraction. All of these objectives focus on social knowledge.

The emphasis in a constructivist program is on logico-mathematical knowledge in the context of autonomy as the broad, long-range goal, that is, the thinking that underlies children's ability to read and write mathematical symbols.

In kindergarten, children can play a game of hiding five (or more) oranges in the room. Half the class hides the oranges and tells the other half how many to look for. The group that looks will have to keep count of how many oranges they have found in order to know how many more to look for.

First graders playing a board game with one die can simply be given a second die and asked how they might play with two dice. The objective here is to encourage children to invent their own ways of adding numbers, rather than "being taught sums." The focus on children's thinking is very different from getting them to write correct answers.

Second graders do not need to be taught rules for double-addition, either. The teacher can just ask how they might problem such as:

$$15$$
$$+17$$

Children who are encouraged to invent their own proced figure out the answer by using their natural ability to think. four examples of their invented procedures:

(a)	(b)	(c)	
$10 + 10 = 20$	$10 + 10 = 20$	$10 + 10 = 20$	1?
$5 + 7 = 12$	$7 + 3 = 10$	$5 + 5 = $ another 10	20
$20 + 10 = 30$	$20 + 10 = 30$	$20 + 10 = 30$	
$30 + 2 = 32$	$30 + 2 = 32$	$30 + 2 = 32$	

Note that the rule (algorithm) that makes children add the ones first and then the tens goes counter to the way children naturally think. Even adults think about 15 as 10 and 5, not as 5 and 10. It is therefore not surprising that children add the tens first. Objectives in mathematics education should be formulated to build on children's natural thinking instead of going counter to it.

To summarize, in traditional mathematics education, social knowledge and lower order skills are primary and logico-mathematical knowledge is incidental. In a constructivist program, logico-mathematical knowledge (higher order thinking) is primary and social knowledge is secondary. When higher test scores become the goals of education because of the looking-good game that grown-ups play, the emphasis on social knowledge and skills becomes even more intense.

How achievement tests influence objectives

Standardized paper-and-pencil tests require the ability to read, write, and understand questions that the teacher reads. Reading, writing, and listening all involve language and therefore social knowledge. When the goal of mathematics education becomes the production of higher test scores, teachers concentrate even more than before on teaching vocabulary and on reading and writing mathematical symbols.

Typical objectives defined by achievement tests include:

- Counting objects (to 20, or by tens)
- Identifying the set with the most members
- Reading two-digit numerals
- Identifying the shape that has been divided into thirds
- Identifying the minus sign as indicative of the operation appropriate to solving a problem
- Adding a column of three one-digit (or two two-digit) numbers
- Identifying the number sentence appropriate to solving an addition problem

Most of these objectives involve social knowledge, and all of them are framed as behavioral objectives. Behaviors can be objectively observed, and social knowledge is easy to measure, but neither induces higher order thinking.

Such test objectives result in another disaster: They put pressure on young children to attain them at ever younger ages. The only way for children to get higher scores is to get more correct answers. The pressure for higher test scores insidiously encourages adults to expect of young children what older children were asked to accomplish several years ago. In fact, today's kindergartners are given the curriculum that used to be considered appropriate for first grade. This results in premature stress and rote learning, to the detriment of children's confidence and foundation for further learning. Teachers know when a question is too hard for their pupils but feel obliged to cover what is on the test, as we saw in Chapter 5 with respect to $4 + \underline{\hspace{1cm}} = 7$ in first grade.

Methods of teaching

Children should be encouraged to develop autonomy, both in the social-moral realm and in the intellectual domain. Exchanges of viewpoints are essential for children's social and moral development as well as for their development of logico-mathematical knowledge (see Chapter 2). It is by exchanging ideas honestly about right and wrong and by making their own decisions that children learn to judge relevant factors and what is morally right. In the intellectual realm, too, children should

Typical tests objectives put pressure on young children to attain these objectives at ever younger ages. The only way for children to get higher scores is to get more correct answers. The pressure for higher test scores insidiously encourages adults to expect of young children what older children were asked to accomplish several years ago. In fact, today's kindergartners are given the curriculum that used to be considered appropriate for first grade. This results in premature stress and rote learning, to the detriment of children's confidence and foundation for further learning. Teachers know when a question is too hard for their pupils but feel obliged to cover what is on the test. Achievement tests measure superficial aspects of mathematics that are easy to measure. The looking-good game that educators play thus creates the illusion of improvement while intensifying the teaching of lower level skills.

be encouraged to invent their own solutions to problems and to come to their own conclusions about the truth of their answers.

Kathy and Mike, introduced at the beginning of this chapter, had their heteronomy regularly reinforced during the math hour, in both the intellectual realm and the social-moral domain. All the initiative came from the teacher. To solve problems such as $27 + 28$, Kathy was told to add the ones first, to write a 5 under the line and a 1 on top of the two 2s, and so on. This was a lesson in obedience: Kathy was learning to become dependent on adults to know how to solve problems and to know whether or not her answers were correct. She was unknowingly being manipulated by rewards such as smiley faces.

Mike never knew when he was successful or not, except through the Cs that appeared on his papers. Because "regrouping" made little sense to him, his confidence in his own ability to think dwindled. His teacher knew that the worksheets were too hard for most of the children in the class, but she had orders from the principal to cover all the materials that were on the test.

Lessons, demonstrations, workbooks, and worksheets can be replaced by classroom activities that encourage intellectual activity and autonomy rather than passivity and heteronomy. Among these are situations in daily living, group games, and discussions of solution procedures invented by children (Kamii, 1982, 1985, 1989a, 1989b; Kamii & DeVries, 1980). These activities will be briefly described.

Daily living

In active classrooms, children are regularly asked to make choices and to vote among alternatives. One day in a first grade classroom, 13 children voted for one of two alternatives, and one boy remarked, "We don't need to vote for the other choice because the 13 already won." The teacher inquired, "How do you know?" and the child explained, "13 and 13 is 26, and we only have 24 kids today." Seeing a sea of blank faces, the teacher asked the rest of the class if they agreed. No, said the others, they needed to count the people who wanted the alternative. When 11 people were counted, the class was satisfied, and the boy who had deduced the outcome commented, "I told you the 13 won."

Life in the classroom is full of arithmetic when the teacher looks for opportunities: choosing leaders of small groups; taking attendance; preparing for snack; distributing materials; counting pieces of games during clean-up; enforcing the number of children allowed in each center (children say, "There's room for one more because six people can paint"). The teacher usually performs these chores, but they can become excellent opportunities for young children to learn arithmetic. Children are proud of being in charge of real responsibilities, and they care about what happens. Problem solving in real-life situations is much more conducive to children's thinking than are pages of exercises repeated with indifference.

Group games

Repetition is necessary for children to learn sums and symbols, and group games offer opportunities to exercise that knowledge. Kindergartners love to play "War." Two children deal an entire deck of regular playing cards, keeping the cards in face-down piles. They both turn over their top cards, and the person with the larger number takes both. Play continues, and the person who collects more cards than the other at the end is the winner. In this context the children repeatedly make comparisons ("more," "less," and "same number"). Other versions of the game exist, and children negotiate to agree on the rules that make the best sense to them.

"Double War" is similar to "War" except that each player turns over two cards on each play (addition), and the person who has the larger total takes all four cards. By playing Double War, children are free to compare combinations such as $2 + 3$ in relation to $2 + 4$. When those combinations turn up, some first graders exclaim that addition is unnecessary since each player has a 2. When $2 + 3$ is to be compared with another combination, $5 + 2$, alert children likewise say that you do not have to add 2 to 5 since $2 + 3 = 5$. When $5 + 8$ is to be compared with $7 + 9$, some children point out that $7 > 5$, and $9 > 8$, thus obviating the need to add.

Instead of having to stop to write the answer to one combination before going on to another, children think critically while playing games. Worksheets that require an answer for every question encourage mechanical counting and writing rather than intelligent strategies. (Furthermore, in the worksheet approach the teacher checks the answers and usually returns the papers the next day. Young children can't remember what they did yesterday and usually don't even care. They are therefore ready to make the same errors all over again.) Additionally, games give children opportunities to learn that they can judge the truth of the answers through their own ability to think.

Children supervise each other while they play games, making sure that the game is played fairly, exchanging opinions, explaining judgments, and enforcing or modifying rules, as when a player takes a peek and chooses a desirable card. They also have to decide what to do when the players get the same total or when the game becomes too easy and boring. In the worksheet approach, children work alone and do not have any opportunity to develop socially or morally.

Finally, the superiority of games over worksheets is illustrated by a phenomenon familiar to all teachers. Some children sit looking out the window until recess time, when the teacher insists that only those who have completed their work can go outside. The fact that these children then finish their work in no time indicates that the worksheets were not intrinsically motivating to them. In comparison, most children beg to play games and do not have to be coerced or bribed to participate.

Discussions of solution strategies

When children get to double-column addition, procedures become harder to invent because numbers have to be taken apart, dealt with separately, and put together. For problems such as $15 + 17$, cited above, traditional mathematics educators teach procedures for producing correct answers. Instead of teaching ready-made rules, it is better to ask children to invent their own solution procedures. They are demonstrably excited and proud of their inventions, such as the four ways described earlier (Kamii, 1989a).

The principles of teaching that the teacher keeps in mind are:

- Encourage children to agree or disagree with each other and refrain from praising right answers or correcting wrong ones.
- Encourage children to think critically and to adopt only the ideas that make sense to them.
- Encourage children to invent many different ways of solving the same problem.

Children who are encouraged to do their own thinking become creative, resourceful, and confident about their own ability to figure things out.

Achievement testing impedes progress in primary mathematics

It is much easier to teach by following the textbook and giving lessons and worksheets than by using daily encounters, games, and discussions of procedures invented by children. To follow a textbook and correct worksheets, the teacher does not need to understand mathematics or children's thinking. By contrast, situations in daily living are not predictable, as when a second grader asked, "Why is this the 20th Century but this is only 1989?" The teacher has to understand second graders' thinking very well to know how to pick up on such a question. Games are also messy, noisy, and more difficult to manage than seatwork. And it must be said that leading discussions can be exhausting, since it is not easy to follow children's thinking.

Achievement testing makes traditional, behavioristic teaching even worse. Since textbooks, workbooks, and worksheets are "aligned" with achievement tests, using them increases the likelihood of higher test scores. To use a constructivist approach, the teacher has to be willing to give up not only an easier way of earning paychecks (though, as any teacher will testify, not an easy way), but also the rewards that come with higher test scores such as merit pay (in some districts) and the respect of peers, administrators, parents, and the community.

Achievement tests measure superficial aspects of mathematics that are easy to measure. The looking-good game that educators play thus creates the illusion of improvement while intensifying the teaching of lower level skills. This is why the National Research Council and the National Council of Teachers of Mathematics insist that unless current evaluation methods are changed, we cannot hope to make reform a reality in mathematics education. The fact that an increasing number of teachers are using a constructivist approach in spite of achievement testing is an indication that we may just be heading in the direction of genuine teacher-led reform.

We are still struggling with the question of how to evaluate children's progress in a constructivist arithmetic program, but decided to put our current thinking on paper in hopes of stimulating exchanges of viewpoints. Three ideas in Chapter 11 impressed us: the idea of "keeping track," that of providing different kinds of information for different audiences from the same raw data, and that of putting teacher judgments at the center of assessment.

Chapter 13

An Approach to Assessment in Mathematics

Constance Kamii and Vasha Rosenblum

This chapter was written to accompany Chapter 11, about the assessment of early literacy. We are still struggling with the question of how to evaluate children's progress in a constructivist arithmetic program but decided to put our current thinking on paper in hopes of stimulating exchanges of viewpoints. Three ideas in Chapter 11 impressed us: the idea of "keeping track," that of providing different kinds of information for different audiences from the same raw data, and that of putting teacher judgments at the center of assessment.

"Keeping track" focuses on children's development from within, over time. It is in sharp contrast with norm-referenced achievement tests that define behavioral objectives. Achievement tests are particularly inadequate in the logico-mathematical realm for educators who are aware of the differences among physical, logico-mathematical, and social knowledge (Chapter 2, pp. 19–20). Since logico-mathematical knowledge develops from within the child, "keeping track" is the only valid way to assess its development.

The idea of providing different kinds of information for different audiences also makes sense. For teachers, specific information about each child is necessary to make decisions about what to teach and how. For example, it is useless for a teacher to find out that a second grader is at the 40th percentile in "Addition With Whole Numbers." On the other hand, specific information such as the fact that a second grader cannot separate 14 into 10 and 4 in his mind is helpful to a teacher. For administrators, however, such details about individual children are not useful. Administrators need quantitative data about groups such as the percentage of second graders who cannot separate 14 mentally into 10 and 4.

The idea of putting teachers in charge of assessment is also a departure from the use of achievement tests. Since teachers have to teach, it makes sense for them to test and observe children systematically. The more precise, in-depth knowledge a teacher has about individual children, the better he or she can teach. To think that paper-and-pencil, multiple choice tests are more scientific or more objective than teacher judgments is pure folly. If teachers are poor observers of children, they should be helped to become better observers rather than being excluded from the assessment process.

Since this chapter is based on the approach described in Chapter 11, we will not repeat the rationale for "keeping track" and for the three levels of evaluation already explained by Engel. We will begin by describing the kinds of primary data (Level One) that the teacher can collect in a constructivist math program (see Chapter 12 and Kamii, 1985, 1989b), and then go on to examples of summaries of individual children's progress (Level Two) and of quantitative information about groups (Level Three). Teachers in traditional math programs can use most of these ideas, such as the observation of children playing games and the place value interview. This chapter will give only examples of a conception of assessment that focuses on children's process of thinking; our aim is not to give recipes or complete sets of items to use.

Level One: Primary data

Socio-moral and attitudinal development

Most people think that the math hour is for children to learn only mathematics. In reality, however, children also learn throughout the day to become able to live autonomously in a democratic society or heteronomously in an autocratic world. For example, Kathy in Chapter 12, who was taught with worksheets and behaviorism, looked highly successful in math, but her heteronomy was reinforced daily. The ability to produce correct answers in math is not worth very much if it is acquired at the expense of socio-moral and attitudinal development. This is one of the reasons why we conceptualize cognitive goals within a socio-moral and attitudinal context and insist that assessment address this context rather than limiting itself to academic subjects.

Some simple ways of assessing children's socio-moral development and confidence in math have already been mentioned in Chapter 2. For example, the teacher can leave the classroom supposedly to get something and tell the class that the teacher across the hall will be keeping an eye on them. If the children continue to work as if the teacher had never left the room, this is a manifestation of socio-moral autonomy. To assess children's confidence in math, a visitor can walk around the classroom while children are completing a worksheet and stop to ask individual children, "How did you get this answer?" (pointing to a correct answer). Many children immediately reach for their erasers, indicating their lack of confidence in their own ideas.

Other methods can be used to assess individual children's socio-moral and attitudinal development. However, we will focus on arithmetic in the rest of this chapter in the interest of brevity.

Development in arithmetic

The teacher can collect data in the classroom in each of the three kinds of activities described in Chapter 12: the use of situations in daily living, games, and teacher-initiated discussions. For "story" problems, it is possible to give paper-and-pencil group tests to first and second graders. Some aspects of arithmetic cannot be assessed in a group, however. For example, kindergartners' construction of number concepts must be assessed in individual interviews. First and second graders' mental arithmetic and their construction of a network of numerical relationships (see Figure 13.1) must also be assessed in individual interviews. Finally, an interview about understanding of place value and "carrying" ("regrouping") is desirable. The collection of some of these data is described below.

Regular classroom activities

Observations in situations in daily living. In kindergarten, the teacher can ask children to take turns setting tables for snacks (cups and napkins). She or he can also ask children to take turns putting the correct number of marbles into a box to choose leaders of small groups. (If children who draw red marbles become leaders, there have to be enough marbles for everyone but as many red ones as leaders.) By systematically observing how children perform these tasks, the teacher can get meaningful, behavioral data.

In first grade, the teacher can ask children to take turns making sure that everybody is accounted for after recording the number present, the number absent, the number ordering lunches, and the number who brought their lunches. In second grade, the teacher can record how individual children count lunch money. The important idea here is systematic observation and recording. Good forms always facilitate recording children's development systematically.

Figure 13.1
Part of a Network of Numerical Relationships*

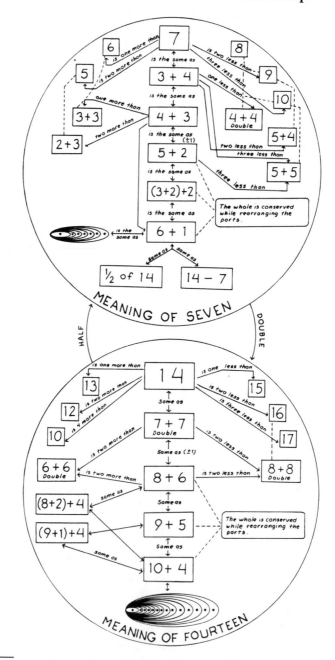

*From *Learning From Children: New Beginnings for Teaching Numerical Thinking* (p. 99) by E. Labinowicz, 1985, Menlo Park, CA: Addison-Wesley. Reproduced by permission of the author.

Observations in group games. Playing games with children is an easy, practical way for the teacher to assess children's numerical reasoning. The teacher can choose a specific game to play with everybody in the class, one or two at a time. The observations must be systematically recorded on a form made for this purpose.

The form in Figure 13.2 evaluates children playing Tens With Playing Cards. This game uses cards 1 through 9. Nine cards are arranged face up in a three-by-three matrix, and a turn consists of taking all the pairs in the matrix that make 10. New cards are added for each subsequent turn. This is a particularly good game in first grade because all first graders can play it at some level, and it taps an important aspect of arithmetic—the ability to make 10 with two numbers.

The teacher records the method the child uses to find combinations that equal 10. When a child "counts-all," he uses the method of counting all the symbols (such as diamonds) on both cards ("1, 2, 3, 4, . . . 10"). A child who "counts-on" starts from the number on one card and counts only the symbols on the second card ("3, 4, 5, 6, . . . 10," for example). A more advanced child will "count-on from the larger" number ("7, 8, 9, 10," for example). The most advanced child will give the combination from memory without counting. The teacher puts a check on the form indicating the number combination and the method used by the child.

Figure 13.2
Observation Form for Tens With Playing Cards

Name _____   Date _____

	Counts-all	Counts-on	Counts-on from larger	Selects without counting (looks for)
$5 + 5$				
$9 + 1$				
$8 + 2$				
$7 + 3$				
$6 + 4$				
Combos $\neq 10$				

A similar game for kindergartners is Fives (Kamii, 1982). Fives uses cards with one, two, three, or four circles on them, and the object of the game is to find two cards that make 5. Many other games can be used to observe children's numerical thinking; each teacher can choose the ones that children like to play and that give the most information.

Observations in discussions of computational procedures. The kind of discussion described in Chapter 12 takes place daily in a constructivist math program in which children are asked to invent their own procedures for double-column addition and other operations. Teachers who conduct these discussions every day know which children can do what from day to day and usually have no trouble filling out the form in Figure 13.3. This figure shows only addition, but teachers can also make forms for multiplication and subtraction.

The emphasis in this form is on the child's process of thinking. In a problem such as $17 + 5$, for example, the child first adds tens as ones (category a, getting 13 for $1 + 7 + 5$ in this case) or adds-on by ones (category b, counting "18, 19, 20, 21, 22"). More advanced procedures are categories c and d. In category c, the child changes $17 + 5$ to $20 + 2$, by taking 3 out of 5 to make 20. In category d, the child separates the double-digit number into tens and ones (10 and 7 in this case), adds the ones ($7 + 5$), makes a ten out of 12, combines the tens ($10 + 10$), and then adds the ones ($20 + 2$).

Some children use instructed methods, or the standard algorithm, either because they have received traditional instruction in other schools or because they have been taught at home. Children's use of the standard algorithm in double-digit addition appears in Figure 13.3 as category 2. We can see in this figure that, on October 5, Brad could add single-digit numbers to double-digit numbers by using his own way of thinking (the "S" entered in Figure 13.3). For the addition of two double-digit numbers, however, Brad was unsuccessful in using a method he had been taught.

Paper-and-pencil group tests

First and second graders can write their solutions to "story" problems and explain their procedures with drawings and "invented" spelling. A difference between this kind of paper-and-pencil test and a standardized achievement test is that only the former informs us about children's process of thinking. When children mark the correct choice in a multiple choice test, we can know only that the answer is correct or

Figure 13.3
Form for Recording Mental Arithmetic in Class (Abridged)

Name **Brad**

	Grading period	1	2	3	4	5	6
	Date of recording	Oct. 5					
Addition **Double-digit plus single-digit (17 + 5)** 1. Invented method a. Adds tens as ones							
b. Adds-on by ones							
c. Changes problem to make multiples of ten		S					
d. Separates tens and ones, adds ones, and makes tens out of ones							
2. Instructed method							
Double-digit plus double-digit (26 + 17) 1. Invented method a. Adds tens as ones							
b. Adds both addends, counting-on by ones							
c. Adds tens only and gets stuck							
d. Adds tens, adds ones, cannot combine							
e. Adds tens, makes tens out of ones, combines tens, and adds ones							
2. Instructed method		U					

"S" stands for "successful"; "U" for "unsuccessful."

incorrect. Furthermore, on an achievement test, the teacher can know only a child's score in "Problem Solving." Without an item analysis about each specific question, it is impossible to know the operation(s) called for and the magnitude of the numbers involved.

Two examples of "story" problems were given in Chapter 2. Another example for second graders is: "The teacher has brought 4 boxes of cookies. There are 23 cookies in each box. How many cookies are there to share all together?" Among the solutions offered by second graders are the following four:

$$\begin{array}{cccc}
\begin{array}{r} 23 \\ \underline{4} \\ 27 \end{array} &
\begin{array}{r} 23 \\ 23 \\ 23 \\ \underline{+23} \\ 92 \end{array} &
\begin{array}{r} 23 \\ 23 \end{array}\!\!\!\begin{array}{l} \\ > 46 \end{array} \\ \begin{array}{r} 23 \\ \underline{23} \end{array}\!\!\!\begin{array}{l} \\ > 46 \\ \underline{} \\ 92 \end{array} &
\begin{array}{r} 23 \\ \underline{\times\ 4} \\ 80 \\ \underline{12} \\ 92 \end{array}
\end{array}$$

The first child added the numbers given in the problem. The second and third children arrived at the correct answer by using addition in two different ways. Only the fourth child used multiplication. While three of the four got the correct answer, the methods they used are far more informative than the simple fact that they got the correct answer.

One way of categorizing children's responses to "story" problems is in terms of the following three levels:

1. Neither the logic nor the answer is correct.
2. The logic is correct, but not the answer.
3. Both the logic and the answer are correct.

The child who added 23 (cookies) and 4 (boxes) in the preceding example would be placed in the first category. The other three children would be placed in the third category. An example of the second category would be the child who wrote $23 + 23 + 23 + 23 = 82$.

Individual interviews

Individual interviews are time consuming but provide specific information about individual children. While a quiet, small room may be ideal, a corner of the classroom is adequate and has the advantage of allowing the teacher to supervise the rest of the class. Our experience indicates that interviews at the beginning, middle, and end of the school year give a good picture of children's progress.

The content of the interview depends on the child's age and range of abilities. In kindergarten, testing for number concepts using the task involving dropping beads into two glasses may be appropriate (see Chapter 2, pp. 17–19). In first grade, we assess children's mental arithmetic with small addends up to $10 + 10$. In second grade, we assess their mental arithmetic in addition, multiplication, and subtraction with one-, or two-, and three-digit numbers. We also assess second graders' understanding of place value and of "carrying" ("regrouping").

Since space is limited and the procedures for the interviews about number concepts and "carrying" have already been described in Chapter 2 (pp. 17–19 and 30–31), we will explain only the interviews with small addends and the place value interview.

Interview with addends up to 10. The purpose of this interview is to determine the extent to which children have begun to construct the kind of network of numerical relationships shown in Figure 13.1. The following materials are used:

For addends up to 6

Two numbered dice

Form for recording responses (see Figure 13.4 and Kamii, 1985, p. 75, for the other questions)

For addends up to 10

Form for recording responses (similar to Figure 13.4; the questions can be found in Kamii, 1985, p. 76)

Ruler

The procedure for assessing the child's ability with addends up to 6 is to begin by showing two 2s on the dice. The teacher asks, "How many points would you get if you rolled these numbers?" and records the child's response on the form. For the second question (5 + 5), the teacher turns the dice so that they both show 5. The teacher records the child's responses in such a way that the interview can later be recreated and analyzed. Verbalizations such as "6-7-8-9-10" are recorded verbatim. For common behaviors, we use codes like those at the top of Figure 13.4. The first two lines in this form show that the child said "four"

Figure 13.4
Form for Recording Mental Arithmetic With Addends
up to 10 (Abridged)

Name _____   Date _____

2 + 2	4
5 + 5	. . . . . F "6-7-8-9-10"
2 + 3	
5 + 4	
4 + 2	
1 + 4	
5 + 6	
3 + 3	
4 + 6	
2 + 6	
6 + 6	
4 + 3	

instantly for $2 + 2$, but that he counted-on after 5 seconds (indicated by five dots), using his fingers in an obvious way (indicated by "F") to do $5 + 5$.

By the time the child gets to addends greater than 6, she can be given a list of questions and asked to use a ruler to show the question she is on and to slide the ruler down after answering each question. In fact, the list of questions and a ruler can be used instead of dice with many first graders in the midyear interview. The analysis of children's responses is discussed later under Level Two.

Place value interview. The interviewer shows a card on which "16" has been written and asks the child to count out 16 chips. The interviewer then circles the 6 of 16 with the back of a pen and asks, "What does *this part* (the 6) mean? Could you show me with the chips what *this part* (the 6) means?" The interviewer then circles the 1 of 16 and asks, "What about *this part* (the 1)? Could you show me with the chips what *this part* (the 1) means?" If the child responds by showing only one chip, the interviewer probes: "You showed me all these chips (pointing out the 16 chips) for this number (circling the 16 on the card), and these (pointing to 6 chips) for this part (circling the 6 on the card), and this chip (pointing) for this part (circling the 1 on the card). What about the rest of the chips (pointing)? Is this how it's supposed to be, or is there something strange here?"

Children's understanding of the 1 of 16 can be categorized as follows:

1. The child shows only one chip (for the 1 in 16).
2. The child changes his or her mind during the interview.
3. The child shows 10 chips immediately with confidence.

Children's notebooks

Children can keep a math notebook to record and work on "story" problems. If they write dates and problems in their notebooks (with "invented" spelling), parents, teachers, and children can later read them and see their progress. (The teacher may prefer to collect some of these pages from time to time.) These kinds of records are much more specific, authentic, and informative for parents and teachers than a percentile rank or grade equivalent about "Problem Solving," which is too vague to mean anything.

In second grade, when some games require paper and pencil for scorekeeping, children can write the date and the name of the game they chose, and record points in their notebooks as they play the game.

By asking children to play certain games during certain weeks, the teacher can collect systematic data about children's ways of showing how many points they got on each turn.

* * *

The primary data described above are all useful in conferences with parents. The specific information collected systematically over time is much more helpful to parents than a letter grade on a report card or numbers on an achievement test. Such letter grades and numbers indicating a child's relative standing in a group do not provide any information about the child's progress or what parents might do to help the child.

It is, of course, not necessary to collect all the data alluded to above. The teacher must decide what kinds of data to collect, and how often, on the basis of various considerations. For example, if the data from a specific game are to be used as "accountability" data, the entire class has to be observed playing the same game at least twice a year. If, however, these data are not to be used as "accountability" data, the teacher can observe each child playing a game appropriate for her or his level of development.

Some teachers may say that the procedures we recommend are too time consuming. However, our procedures take only a small fraction of the time required by worksheets, test preparation, and the repeated reviews that are now taking place in most classrooms. The teachers we work with say that they learn much more about children's numerical thinking by playing math games with children than by correcting worksheets. The assessment procedures we recommend thus require rethinking teaching and learning in a fundamental way, rather than merely replacing achievement tests with another instrument.

Level Two: Summaries of individual children's progress

Good forms facilitate keeping track of children's progress in arithmetic. Below are a few examples of the use of forms presented in Figures 13.2, 13.3, and 13.4.

Progress in games

To keep track of progress in a game, all we have to do is to fill out the same form a few times during the year, such as the one presented in Figure 13.2. Progress can be seen in the movement of check marks from left to right, from the column labeled "Counts-all" to the one entitled "Selects without counting (looks for)," and downward, from 5 + 5 and 9 + 1 to 6 + 4.

Progress in discussions of computational procedures

The form presented in Figure 13.3 will show each child's progress or lack of progress from one grading period to another. Within the "invented method" section of each category, the level of thinking generally advances as the child descends from *a* to *d* or *e*. By examining the entries in the unabridged form, the teacher can see when the child became successful in subtraction and multiplication, and whether the child is thinking in terms of ones, tens, or both.

Progress in addition with addends up to 10

Since our objective in single-digit addition is that children construct a network of numerical relationships (see Figure 13.1), we use the speed of correct responses as an indicator of a numerical relationship. (However, we never give timed tests or tell children that they have to respond quickly.) We first circle in red on the record sheet (Figure 13.4) all the

Figure 13.5
Summary Sheet for Mental Arithmetic With Addends
up to 10 (Abridged)

	September	January	May
2 + 2			
5 + 5			
2 + 3			
5 + 4			
4 + 2			
1 + 4			
5 + 6			
3 + 3			
4 + 6			
2 + 6			
6 + 6			
4 + 3			

correct responses made within 5 seconds without any evidence of counting. We then take a summary sheet (Figure 13.5) and enter a "+" for each item that has a red circle around it. By inspecting the +'s entered on the summary sheet in September, January, and May, the teacher, parents, and child can quickly see the progress made over the school year.

Level Three: Quantitative information about groups

The most useful data for administrators and the public are percentages and averages about each class or grade level. Examples of how to change Level One primary data into quantitative information are given below.

Progress in games

A first grade teacher can count the checks in the last column of Figure 13.2 and give the percentages of children in the class who selected each combination from memory. Below is an example of how the percentages may be presented for September and May:

Combinations that make 10	Percentage of children who knew without counting	
	September	*May*
5 + 5	68	100
9 + 1	64	100
8 + 2	20	88
7 + 3	4	84
6 + 4	4	68

Progress in discussions of computational procedures

A second grade teacher can count the number in category 1.*e* of "double-digit plus double-digit (26 + 17)" in Figure 13.3 and report the percentages of children in this category. Below is an example of how the data might be presented for October and May:

	October	*May*
Solves 26 + 17 by adding tens, making tens out of ones, combining tens, and adding ones.	20%	84%

The primary data described in this chapter are all useful in conferences with parents. The specific information collected systematically over time is much more helpful to parents than a letter grade on a report card or numbers on an achievement test. Such letter grades and numbers indicating a child's relative standing in a group do not provide any information about the child's progress or what parents might do to help the child.

Progress in "story" problems

If the teacher gives the same "story" problem twice a year, progress is easy to determine by comparing percentages. For example, the problem about four boxes of cookies may yield the following percentages:

	September	May
1. Neither the logic nor the answer is correct $(23 + 4 = 27)$.	70%	10%
2. The logic is correct, but not the answer $(23 + 23 + 23 + 23 = 82)$.	20%	30%
3. Both the logic and the answer are correct $(23 + 23 + 23 + 23 = 92)$.	10%	60%

Progress in addition with addends up to 10

This analysis is done is two phases consisting of (1) making three summary sheets for the class—one in September, one in January, and one in May—and (2) making a summary sheet for the class for the entire year. The summary sheet shown in Figure 13.5 is used differently in both of these phases.

To make a summary sheet for the class for the September interviews, the teacher uses the summary sheet shown in Figure 13.5 and replaces the three wide columns for September, January, and May with a narrow column for each child in the class. Two extra columns are added: one for the total number of +'s for the class (labeled "Total") and the other for the percentages of +'s (labeled "%").

The teacher then refers to each child's summary sheet (Figure 13.5) and enters +'s in the appropriate spaces on the class summary sheet for September. When all the +'s have been entered for all the children in the class, the teacher counts the number of +'s for each item (such as $2 + 2$) and records the total for that item in the "Total" column. After completing this column for all the items, she converts each of these numbers into a percentage and records it in the "%" column. These are the numbers that let administrators and the public know that in September, 92% of a first-grade class knew $2 + 2$, 68% knew $5 + 5$, and so on.

The teacher repeats the same procedure in January, and again in May, to get the percentage of +'s for each item each time.

The second phase, that of making a summary sheet for the class for the entire year, is much simpler. The teacher uses the summary sheets shown in Figure 13.5, with the same three columns for September,

January, and May. However, instead of entering +'s for each child, she enters the percentages of +'s for the entire class. In other words, the teacher records the percentages from the "%" column of each of the three class summary sheets made in September, January, and May. The same information about the progress of the class can be presented in graph form as in Figure 11.3.

Conclusion

The assessment procedures described in this chapter give much more specific information than norm-referenced achievement tests and focus on children's thinking rather than on correct answers and superficial social knowledge. However, these procedures can quickly become as misleading to adults and harmful to children as achievement tests if grown-ups continue to play the looking-good game. As long as teachers feel pressured by administrators, parents, and the public to produce higher numbers, they will feel compelled to drill children.

Children can be drilled to say "10" when they see 6 + 4, or they can come to remember this combinaton for themselves as they play games and put 6 + 4 into relationship with 5 + 5. Children can also be drilled to give correct answers in double-column addition, without understanding what they are doing (see the discussion of Table 2.1.) However, they can also be encouraged to invent their own procedures that make sense to them. If the pressure of the looking-good game remains high, teachers will surely resort to behavioristic teaching methods that produce quick results.

When a second grader cannot mentally separate 14 into 10 and 4, it is the fault neither of the child nor of the teacher that this is an impossibility for him. In the logico-mathematical realm, it is especially important to give children the time they need to construct a solid foundation for future growth from within.

Behavioristic attempts to improve test scores and other numbers are like efforts to lower a patient's temperature while leaving the underlying cause of an illness untouched. Tools such as thermometers, achievement tests, and procedures to "keep track" can be used in an informed, honest manner for children's benefit or in the service of grown-ups' looking-good game.

Chapter 14

Conclusion: What Educators and Others Can Do

Constance Kamii

Attempts to make schools accountable through achievement testing have resulted in "doing more of what has not been working, and doing it earlier in children's lives" (Lilian Katz, personal communication, March 1989). Many forces have contributed to this state of affairs, and we saw in the preceding chapters that thoughtful superintendents, principals, teachers, teacher educators, and curriculum consultants in state departments of education feel caught up and frustrated in the interplay of the games grown-ups play.

Test-driven instruction would not dominate the classroom if more superintendents educated their school boards about the inappropriateness of achievement tests, if more principals studied how children learn, and if more teachers insisted on doing what is good for young children's development. Madaus (1988) points out that the power of high-stakes testing is "a perceptual phenomenon: if students, teachers, or administrators believe that the results of an examination are important, it matters very little whether this is really true or false" (p. 88). As in the story about the emperor's new clothes, if "experts" think test scores are important, others will share this belief. Early childhood educators must critically examine facts and theories and not be dazzled by tests just because they look scientific or because governors, legislators, and community leaders believe that tests reveal "the truth" about children's learning.

At their annual meeting in 1989, the National Association of Elementary School Principals (NAESP) adopted a resolution expressing reservations over the practice of mandating a certain achievement test score for promotion to a higher grade. The resolution also calls for multiple and varied assessment procedures and use of test scores "in ways that benefit children" rather than in punitive ways (NAESP, 1989). In a report soon to be issued, NAESP echos the National Association of

State Boards of Education (cited in the Introduction of this book) and argues against practices such as standardized testing, kindergarten retention, and "transitional" programs for kindergarten and first grade children considered not "ready" for regular classes. The principals' report urges schools to adapt to children's needs and be ready to receive children as they come, rather than adopting kindergarten programs that look more and more like first grade and labeling children as "ready" or "not ready" for kindergarten.

The pendulum has swung back and forth between what has come to be called "social" promotion and the promotion only of those who are "ready" for the next grade. Putting a stop to swinging between practices that have never worked before is long overdue. It may seem sensible to retain children in grade unless they are "ready," but as Smith and Shepard (1987) point out:

> The body of evidence addressing this assumption . . . is almost uniformly negative. Indeed, few collections of educational research are so unequivocal. The most comprehensive of the several reviews of research on retention is a meta-analysis conducted by Thomas Holmes and Kenneth Matthews (1984). The consistent conclusion of such reviews is that children make progress during the year in which they repeat a grade, *but not as much progress* as similar children who were promoted. In controlled studies of the effect of nonpromotion on both achievement and personal adjustment, children who repeat a grade are consistently worse off than comparable children who are promoted with their age-mates. Contrary to popular belief, the average negative effect of retention on achievement is *even greater* than the negative effect on emotional adjustment and self-concept. (p. 130)

The reason for the ineffectiveness of retention is that children are not empty vessels that can be filled by pouring knowledge into them. Children learn by constructing knowledge from the inside, and if attempts to transmit knowledge did not work during one year, it is unlikely that the same method of teaching will work the next year. Only by designing educational programs cognizant of *how* children learn can we ensure that children *will* learn (Bredekamp, 1987; Peck, McCaig, & Sapp, 1988). Educators have to lead education rather than simply doing what the public wants.

Photo p. 165: *Attempts to make schools accountable through achievement testing have resulted in doing more of what has not been working, and doing it earlier in children's lives. Test-driven instruction would not dominate the classroom if more superintendents educated their school boards about the inappropriateness of achievement tests, if more principals studied how children learn, and if more teachers insisted on doing what is good for young children's development.*

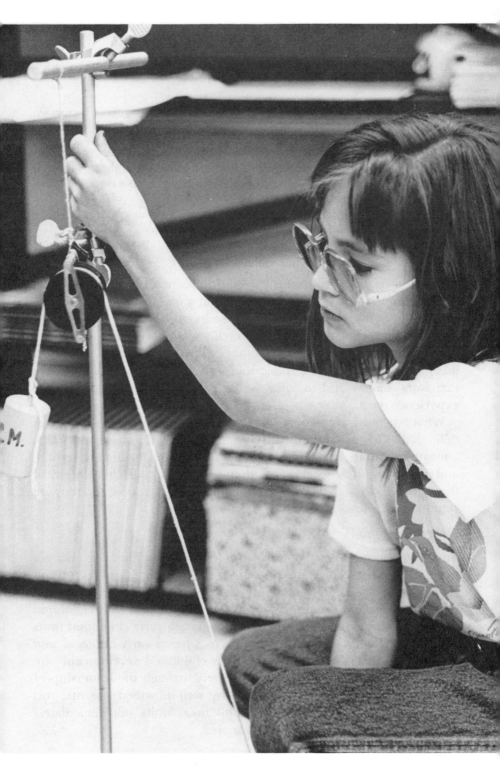

What educators can do

A bold venture by a group of high school seniors suggests a lesson we can learn.

> Some seniors at West High School in Torrance, Calif., came up with a . . . strategy for signaling their agreement with the contention that schools are placing too much emphasis on standardized tests.
>
> Instead of confining their frustration to articles in newspapers or education journals, they went straight to its source, deliberately flunking the California Assessment Program tests. ("Student Saboteurs," 1989, p. 3)

This is a strategy grown-ups have not thought about. If all teachers likewise stopped playing the looking-good game through agreements reached at state-level professional meetings, the negative effects of achievement testing on classroom practices would stop immediately.

While this strategy has the advantage of direct and immediate results, it is not a permanently desirable solution. It would continue to waste taxpayers' money and to force young children to undergo a failure experience once a year.

What we need are short- and long-term goals that can be better defended, such as administratively separating early childhood units, educating parents, changing laws and regulations mandating testing, and improving the education of administrators and teachers. Many of these goals have been discussed in the preceding chapters, and they are summarized below.

Short-term goals

Administratively separating early childhood units. The two changes proposed by the National Association of State Boards of Education (1988) are (1) the establishment of separate facilities for children 4 to 8 years of age, each with a principal knowledgeable about early childhood education, or (2) the establishment of separate early childhood units within elementary schools, each with "a *separate early childhood unit director* with specialized training in early childhood development" (p. 10). These steps can be taken immediately through the leadership of local superintendents. If supported by well-informed parents, this administrative separation of early childhood units will immediately reduce the pressure for higher test scores.

Educating parents. Parents care the most about their own children's welfare. However, the great majority honestly believe that achievement tests are valid and that worksheets are educational. When teachers and principals are informed enough and convinced enough that children learn better by interacting with objects and people, most parents come to new understandings with surprising speed. After all, parents know what children mean when they begin to ask, "Do I *have* to go to school today?" Teachers and principals can inform parents in individual conferences and school-level meetings.

When parents become convinced of the undesirability of achievement testing and worksheets, they can be powerful allies in the political process. Because their own children are involved, they are willing to mount campaigns to influence school board members, legislators, and other elected officials. Interestingly enough, those who impose accountability on others are never held accountable. They do not have to prove through scientific research and theory that their mandates benefit children.

Changing laws and regulations. For five years, the North Carolina Assocation for the Education of Young Children and the Atlantic Center for Research in Education (ACRE) worked for passage of legislation (in 1987) outlawing standardized testing in first and second grades. This campaign, led by Page McCullough, former director of ACRE, serves as a shining example of what educators can accomplish by educating themselves, legislators, parents, the media, and voters about the ill effects of achievement testing on young children's development.

Another organized effort is the Community for Effective Student Evaluation (CESE) in Arizona, led by Ann Gould. Through persistent work, this group succeeded in getting the Arizona legislature to pass a bill limiting mandatory first grade testing to a sample of students.

In 1989, the Texas legislature and governor were also persuaded to eliminate the Texas Educational Assessment of Minimal Skills test from first grade, and Texas does not require a second grade test. In Wisconsin, a bill under consideration, modeled after the North Carolina testing ban, states that "a school board may not administer standardized tests to pupils in kindergarten to grade 2" (National Center for Fair and Open Testing, 1989, p. 13). In Mississippi, the Department of Education decided in 1988 to discontinue standardized testing of kindergarten children, and in Georgia, the State Board of Education dropped a test that had been used in 1988 to determine entry into first grade. These moves away from achievement testing happened because of the insistence of educators, parents, and other advocates for young children. State affiliates of the National Association for the Education of Young Children can likewise become powerful political forces.

Political action takes years of hard work because it is not easy to persuade legislators, boards of education, and the public that achievement tests give misleading information about young children's learning and that test-driven instruction focuses only on surface skills that are easy to measure. Political action also takes time because most educators do not know how legislative bodies and state boards of education work, and most of us are naive about vote-getting games.

An organization prepared to assist in political and legal efforts is the National Center for Fair and Open Testing (FairTest), located in Cambridge, Massachusetts. In March 1989, FairTest cosponsored the Southern Regional Conference on Testing Reform with 10 other organization such as the Alabama Association for Young Children, the Kentucky Association on Children Under Six, the Louisiana Association for the Education of Young Children, and the Oklahoma Association on Children Under Six. This was the beginning of the Southern Network on Testing Reform, which promises to grow and follow the examples set in North Carolina and Arizona. FairTest also cosponsored a conference in New York City in May 1989 on emerging techniques in alternative literacy evaluation.

Increasingly, educators and journalists are calling for changes in the laws and regulations mandating achievement testing. Many educators at all grade levels are saying that achievement tests are too limited to serve as measures of accountability, and that merely raising standards for promotion to the next grade aggravates the dropout problem and the inequality among minority groups. *Phi Delta Kappan* has consistently published articles critical of quick fixes and devoted a special section to testing in its May 1989 issue. The Association for Supervision and Curriculum Development focused its April 1989 issue of *Educational Leadership* on the theme "Redirecting Assessment." *The New York Times*, too, periodically reports on testing: "A Mania For Testing Spells Money" (October 16, 1988) and "Debate Intensifying on Screening Tests Before Kindergarten" (May 11, 1989). Other newspapers have published articles with headlines such as "Public School Tests Called Excessive" (*San Francisco Chronicle*, June 14, 1988), "Some Schools Press So Hard Kids Become Stressed and Fearful" (*The Wall Street Journal*, July 16, 1988), and "Teachers Tell of Pressure To Raise Student Scores" (*Los Angeles Times*, September 2, 1988).

Public opinion may be more ready today to hear why achievement testing should be banned in grades K – 2. Groups likely to be helpful are early childhood specialists in state departments of education and universities. These groups are generally opposed to achievement and "readiness" testing, but work outside school systems and bodies that mandate standardized testing.

Long-term goals

Improving the preparation of administrators. In hospitals, physicians, not administrators, make decisions about medical practices. Hospital administrators' role is to facilitate the work of doctors, who have the scientific training necessary to make decisions about treatments. In schools, by contrast, administrators have the power to make curriculum decisions, but they are not required to know child development or to keep up with research about teaching and learning. Generally, superintendents know less about child development, learning, and teaching than principals, and many elementary school principals in turn know less about these than teachers of young children. Administrators are required to take many courses about the financial, legal, and administrative aspects of schools but not about how children develop and learn.

In a sharply worded document entitled *Improving the Preparation of School Administrators: An Agenda for Reform,* the National Policy Board for Educational Administration (1989) called for a total overhaul of how administrators are recruited, trained, and licensed and certified. The Board consists of the presidents and executive secretaries of 10 prestigious organizations such as the American Association of School Administrators, the Association for Supervision and Curriculum Development, the Council of Chief State School Officers, the National Association of Elementary School Principals, the National Council of Professors of Educational Administration, and the National School Boards Association. Among its recommendations is the proposal that all administrators possess a master's degree in teaching and evidence of successful teaching in classrooms, arguing that "the teaching and learning process is the core function of the school" (p. 14). If implemented, this will be a major step toward administrator's becoming knowledgeable about teaching and learning.

Improving teacher education. If teachers have reluctantly followed the bandwagon of achievement testing, it is an outcome of the education they have received. In medicine, physicians cannot be forced en masse to do what is harmful to their patients. A difference between medicine and education is that, in schools, the effects of malpractice are not detected by most parents or even teachers. The major difference between physicians' professional conscience and teachers' is, however, that education is still a prescientific field, and most teachers were not educated to base their practices on scientific explanations. In medicine, cancer is not yet explained, and physicians know that they can treat only the symptoms. In education, by contrast, many teachers are not clear in their minds about the difference between drilling children on surface behaviors (that is, symptoms) and fostering the construction of knowledge from within. Many do not know the difference between memorizing spelling words and making progress in "invented" spelling (see Chapter 2). As far as number concepts are concerned, the great majority have not even heard of logico-mathematical, social, and physical knowledge (see Chapter 2).

Achievement tests are scientific tools made with extensive research. However, science does not come ready made and fully grown, and all sciences develop by going through one stage after another of being "wrong." Just as astronomers before Copernicus had to work within the framework of the geocentric theory, psychologists had to go through a primitive stage of associationism, behaviorism, and psychometric tests. All sciences begin by studying surface, observable phenomena, and it is not suprising that psychologists began by focusing on animals' behaviors and human beings' lower order skills. As discussed in Chapter 2, a broader, more powerful theory came later to explain the development of autonomy in human beings, both in the intellectual and morals realms.

If it took 150 years for the heliocentric theory to become universally accepted, it is not surprising that constructivism remains unknown and/or unaccepted decades after the publication of *The Moral Judgment of the Child* (Piaget, 1932/1965), *The Construction of Reality in the Child* (Piaget, 1937/1954), *The Child's Conception of Number* (Piaget & Szeminska, 1941/1952), *The Child's Conception of Time* (Piaget, 1946/1969), and *The Child's Conception of Space* (Piaget & Inhelder, 1948/1956).

Test mania is a stage that American education had to go through because teachers and administrators are not trained to understand the relationships among behaviorism, associationism, and constructivism or how achievement tests are made (see Chapters 1 and 2). Without such training, it is easy to be dazzled by the scientific appearance of

The National Association of Elementary School Principals (NAESP) has adopted a resolution expressing reservations over the practice of mandating a certain achievement test score for promotion to a higher grade. The resolution also calls for multiple and varied assessment procedures and use of test scores in ways that benefit children rather than in punitive ways. NAESP echoes the National Association of State Boards of Education and argues against practices such as standardized testing, kindergarten retention, and "transitional" programs for kindergarten and first grade children considered not "ready" for regular classes. The principals' report urges schools to adapt to children's needs and be ready to receive children as they come, rather than adopting kindergarten programs that look more and more like first grade and labeling children as "ready" or "not ready" for kindergarten.

these tests and to feel unequipped to oppose their misuse. About half of the principals in Morgan-Worsham's survey (see Chapter 5) believed that achievement tests are not valid in grades K–2, and I am sure the percentage of this opinion is much higher among teachers of young children.

It is unfortunate that such large proportions of teachers and principals are cowed into drilling children to produce results that they know are counterproductive. Teacher educators must educate future teachers to become more autonomous. Critical, independent thinking, a goal of education discussed for children in Chapter 2, should also be a goal for teacher education. Educators' heteronomy is an outcome of traditional education that unwittingly promotes obedience and conformity. In addition to intellectual autonomy, teacher educators must strive to develop moral autonomy in teachers and administrators. "I am only following orders" and "Everybody else is doing it" are not acceptable excuses, especially for educators.

The nation's schools do need improvement. However, we will not turn out intelligent, literate, or moral citizens by giving tests to children and training them to do well on tests. Many educators such as John Dewey have amply demonstrated that children learn for themselves when they are personally involved and committed to activities that are meaningful to them. Young children are curious and come to school eager to learn. Educators' task is to build on this natural motivation, rather than imposing standards that run counter to the ways in which young children learn.

References

Allington, R. L. (1983). The reading instruction provided readers of different reading abilities. *The Elementary School Journal, 83,* 548–559.

Association for Supervision and Curriculum Development. (1987). Testing concerns. In *Forty years of leadership: A synthesis of ASCD resolutions through 1987* (pp. 17–19). Alexandria, VA: Author.

Baker, E. L., Burstein, L., Linn, R. L., & Shepard, L. (1989, March). *Cannell revisited: Accountability, test score gains, normative comparisons, and achievement.* Paper presented at the meeting of the American Educational Research Association, San Francisco.

Bamberger, J., Ferreiro, E., Frey-Streiff, M., & Sinclair, A. (1988). *La production de notations chez le jeune enfant* [The production of notations in the young child]. Paris: Presses Universitaires de France.

Barbour, N., Webster, T. D., & Drosdeck, S. (1987). Sand: A resource for the language arts. *Young Children, 42*(2), 20–25.

Bissex, G. (1980). *GYNS AT WRK: A child learns to write and read.* Cambridge, MA: Harvard University Press.

Bredekamp, S. (Ed.). (1987). *Developmentally appropriate practice in early childhood programs serving children from birth through age 8* (expanded ed.). Washington, DC: NAEYC.

Bredekamp, S., & Shepard, L. (1989). How best to protect children from inappropriate school expectations, practices, and policies. *Young Children, 44*(3), 14–24.

Brigance, A. H. (1982). *Brigance K and 1 Screen for Kindergarten and First Grade.* North Billerica, MA: Curriculum Associates, Inc.

Calkins, L. M. (1986). *The art of teaching writing.* Portsmouth, NH: Heinemann.

Cannell, J. J. (1987). *Nationally normed elementary achievement testing in America's public schools: How all fifty states are above the national average.* Daniels, WV: Friends for Education.

Cawelti, G. (1988, June). Better measures of student achievement called for. *ASCD Update,* p. 2.

Clay, M. (1979). *The early detection of reading difficulties: A diagnostic survey with recovery procedures.* Auckland, New Zealand: Heinemann Educational Books.

Coles, G. (1987). *The learning mystique: A critical look at "learning disabilities."* New York: Pantheon.

Connell, D. R. (1987). The first 30 years were the fairest: Notes from the kindergarten and ungraded primary (K–1–2). *Young Children, 42*(5), 30–39.

DeVries, R., & Kohlberg, L. (1987). *Programs of early education.* New York: Longman.

Dorsey, A. G. (1988). *Early childhood teacher educators' survey.* Unpublished manuscript.

Dossey, J. A., Mullis, I. V. S., Lindquist, M. M., & Chambers, D. L. (1988). *The mathematics report card: Are we measuring up?* Princeton: Educational Testing Service.

Duckworth, E. (1987). *The having of wonderful ideas and other essays on teaching and learning.* New York: Teachers College Press, Columbia University.

Durkins, D. (1966). *Children who read early.* New York: Teachers College Press, Columbia University.

Edelsky, C., & Draper, K. (in press). Reading/"reading"; writing/"writing"; text/"text." In A. Petrosky (Ed.), *Reading and writing: Theory and research.* Norwood, NJ: Ablex.

Edelsky, C., & Smith, K. (1984). Is that writing—or are those marks just a figment of your curriculum? *Language Arts, 61,* 24–32.

Ferreiro, E., & Teberosky, A. (1982). *Literacy before schooling.* Portsmouth, NH: Heinemann. (Original work published 1979)

Gartrell, D. (1987). Punishment or guidance? *Young Children, 42*(3), 55–61.

Gesell Institute of Human Development. (1980). *Gesell School Readiness Test.* Rosemont, NJ: Programs for Education.

Goodlad, J. I. (1984). *A place called school.* New York: McGraw-Hill.

Goodman, K. S. (1979). Miscues: Windows on the reading process. In K. S. Goodman (Ed.), *Miscue analysis: Applications to reading instruction* (p. 5). Urbana, IL: ERIC Clearinghouse on Reading and Communication Skills.

Goodman, K. (1986). *What's whole in whole language?* Portsmouth, NH: Heinemann.

Goodman, K., Shannon, P., Freeman, Y., & Murphy, S. (1988). *Report card on basal readers.* Katonah, NY: Richard C. Owen.

Gordon, T. (1975). *Teacher effectiveness training.* New York: McKay.

Graves, D. H. (1982). *Writing: Teachers and children at work.* Portsmouth, NH: Heinemann.

Greenberg, P. (in press). *Encouraging self-esteem and self-discipline: Character development—infancy through age 8.* Washington, DC: NAEYC.

Haney, W., & Madaus, G. (1989). Searching for alternatives to standardized tests: Whys, whats, and whithers. *Phi Delta Kappan, 70,* 683–687.

Harste, J. C., Woodward, V. A., & Burke, C. L. (1984). *Language stories and literacy lessons.* Portsmouth, NH: Heinemann.

Hendrick, J. (1988). *The whole child: Developmental education for the early years* (4th ed.). Columbus, OH: Merrill.

Hirsch, E. S. (Ed.). (1984). *The block book* (rev. ed.). Washington, DC: NAEYC.

Holdaway, D. (1979). *The foundation of literacy.* Sydney, Australia: Ashton Scholastic.

Holmes, C. T., & Matthews, K. M. (1984). The effects of nonpromotion on elementary and junior high school pupils. *Review of Educational Research, 54,* 225–236.

Holt, B. (1989). *Science with young children* (rev. ed.). Washington, DC: NAEYC.

Hubbard, R. (1987). Transferring images: Not just glued on the page. *Young Children, 42*(2), 60–67.

Hubbard, R. (1988). Allow children's individuality to emerge in their writing: Let their voices through. *Young Children, 43*(3), 33–38.

Inhelder, B., & Piaget, J. (1963). De l'itération des actions à la récurrence élémentaire [From the repetition of actions to elementary iteration]. In P. Gréco, B. Inhelder, B. Matalon, & J. Piaget, *La formation des raisonnements récurrentiels* (pp. 47–120). Paris: Presses Universitaires de France.

Kamii, C. (1982). *Number in preschool and kindergarten.* Washington, DC: NAEYC.

Kamii, C. (1984). Autonomy: The aim of education envisioned by Piaget. *Phi Delta Kappan, 65,* 410–415.

Kamii, C. (1985). *Young children reinvent arithmetic.* New York: Teachers College Press, Columbia University.

Kamii, C. (1989a). *Double-column addition: A teacher uses Piaget's theory* [Videotape]. New York: Teachers College Press, Columbia University.

Kamii, C. (1989b). *Young children continue to reinvent arithmetic — Second grade.* New York: Teachers College Press, Columbia University.

Kamii, C., & DeVries, R. (1980). *Group games in early education: Implications of Piaget's theory.* Washington, DC: NAEYC.

Katz, L. (1986, November). Panel presentation at the meeting of the National Association for the Education of Young Children, Washington, DC.

Kennedy, M. M. (1987). Inexact sciences: Professional education and the development of expertise. In E. Z. Rothkopf (Ed.), *Review of research in education* (Vol. 14, pp. 133–167). Washington, DC: American Educational Research Association.

Kohlberg, L., & Mayer, R. (1972). Development as the aim of education, *Harvard Educational Review, 42*, 449–496.

Kontos, S. (1986). What preschool children know about reading how they learn it. *Young Children, 42*(1), 58–66.

Labinowicz, E. (1985). *Learning from children: New beginnings for teaching numerical thinking.* Menlo Park, CA: Addison-Wesley.

Leinwand, S. (1985). Coping with the pressures of standardized math tests. *Learning, 13*(6), 26–30.

Leinwand, S. (1986). Curricular improvement versus standardized testing. *The Arithmetic Teacher, 33*(8), 3.

Madaus, G. F. (1988). The influence of testing on the curriculum. In L. N. Tanner (Ed.), *Critical issues in curriculum: 87th yearbook of the National Society for the Study of Education* (pp. 83–121). Chicago: University of Chicago Press.

Manning, M., Long, R., Manning, G., & Kamii, C. (1987, April). *Spelling in kindergarten.* Paper presented at the meeting of the American Educational Research Association, Washington, DC.

Mathematical Sciences Education Board. (1988). *A framework for revision of K–12 mathematics curricula* (draft). Washington, DC: National Research Council.

McDermott, R. P., & Aron, J. (1978). Pirandello in the classroom: On the possibility of equal educational opportunity in American culture. In M. C. Reynolds (Ed.), *Futures of education for exceptional students: Emerging structures* (pp. 41–64). Reston, VA: Council for Exceptional Children.

Meisels, S. J. (1989). High-stakes testing in kindergarten. *Educational Leadership, 46*(7), 16–22.

Nachbar, R. R. (1989). A K/1 class can work—wonderfully! *Young Children, 44*(5), 67–71.

National Association for the Education of Young Children. (1988a). NAEYC position statement on standardized testing of young children 3 through 8 years of age. *Young Children, 43*(3), 42–47.

National Association for the Education of Young Children. (1988b). *Testing of young children: Concerns and cautions.* Washington, DC: Author.

National Association of Early Childhood Teacher Educators. (1989). Resolution: Testing in the early years. *The Journal of Early Childhood Teacher Education, 10*(1), 16–17.

National Association of Elementary School Principals. (1989). Standardized tests. In *Platform 1988–1989* (p. 7). Alexandria, VA: Author.

National Association of State Boards of Education. (1988). *Right from the start.* Alexandria, VA: Author.

National Center for Fair and Open Testing. (1989, Summer). States move on testing reform. *FairTest Examiner*, pp. 1, 13.

National Commission on Excellence in Education. (1983). *A nation at risk: The imperative for educational reform.* Washington, DC: U. S. Government Printing Office.

National Council of Teachers of English. (1989). Testing and evaluation. In *NCTE forum: Position statements on issues in education from the National Council of Teachers of English* (pp. VI:1 – VI:4). Urbana, IL: Author.

National Council of Teachers of Mathematics. (1989). *Curriculum and evaluation standards for school mathematics*. Reston, VA: Author.

National Policy Board for Educational Administration. (1989). *Improving the preparation of school administrators: An agenda for reform*. Charlottesville, VA: Author (at University of Virginia Curry School of Education).

National Research Council. (1989). *Everybody counts: A report to the nation on the future of mathematics education*. Washington, DC: National Academy Press.

Newman, J.M. (1985). *Whole language: Theory in use*. Portsmouth, NH: Heinemann.

Ohanian, S. (1984). Standardized tests versus true learning. *Educational Digest, 50*(4), 40 – 42.

Peck, J. T., McCaig, G., & Sapp, M. E. (1988). *Kingergarten policies: What is best for children?* Washington, DC: NAEYC.

Perrone, V. (1977). *Standardized testing and evaluation*. Wheaton, MD: Association for Childhood Education International.

Piaget, J. (1954). *The construction of reality in the child* (M. Cook, Trans.). New York: Basic. (Original work published 1937)

Piaget, J. (1965). *The moral judgment of the child* (M. Gabain, Trans.). New York: Free Press. (Original work published 1932)

Piaget, J. (1969). *The child's conception of time* (A. J. Pomerans, Trans.). London: Routledge & Kegan Paul. (Original work published 1946)

Piaget, J. (1973). *To understand is to invent* (G. Roberts, Trans.). New York: Viking. (Original work published 1948)

Piaget, J., & Inhelder, B. (1956). *The child's conception of space* (F. J. Langdon & J. L. Lunzer, Trans.). London: Routledge & Kegan Paul. (Original work published 1948)

Piaget, J., & Szeminska, A. (1952). *The child's conception of number* (C. Gattegno & F. M. Hodgson, Trans.). London: Routledge & Kegan Paul. (Original work published 1941)

Ripple, R.E., & Rockcastle, V.N. (Eds.). (1964). *Piaget rediscovered*. Ithaca, NY: Cornell University School of Education.

Rist, R. (1973). *The urban school: A factory for failure*. Cambridge, MA: MIT Press.

Sawyers, J. K., & Rogers, C. S. (1988). *Helping young children develop through play: A practical guide for parents, caregivers, and teachers*. Washington, DC: NAEYC.

Schickedanz, J. A. (1986). *More than the ABCs: The early stages of reading and writing*. Washington, DC: NAEYC.

Seefeldt, C. (1980). *Teaching young children*. Englewood Cliffs, NJ: Prentice-Hall.

Seefeldt, C., & Barbour, N. (1988). "They said I had to . . ." Working with mandates. *Young Children, 43*(4), 4 – 8.

Shepard, L. (1987, January). *The assessment of readiness for school: Psychometric and other considerations*. Presentation at the National Center for Educational Statistics, Washington, DC.

Smith, F. (1971). *Understanding reading: A psycholinguistic analysis of reading and learning to read*. New York: Holt, Rinehart & Winston.

Smith, F. (1973). *Psycholinguistics and reading.* New York: Holt, Rinehart & Winston.

Smith, F. (1975). *Comprehension and learning: A conceptual framework for teachers.* New York: Holt, Rinehart & Winston.

Smith, F. (1983). *Essays into literacy.* Portsmouth, NH: Heinemann.

Smith, F. (1985). *Reading without nonsense* (2nd ed.). New York: Teachers College Press, Columbia University.

Smith, F. (1986). *Insult to intelligence: The bureaucratic invasion of our classrooms.* New York: Arbor House.

Smith, F. (1988). *Understanding reading* (4th ed.). Hillsdale, NJ: Erlbaum.

Smith, M. L., & Shepard, L. A. (1987). What doesn't work: Explaining policies of retention in the early grades. *Phi Delta Kappan, 69,* 129–134.

Stone, J. G. (1978). *A guide to discipline* (rev. ed.). Washington, DC: NAEYC.

Strickland, D. S., & Morrow, L. M. (Eds.). (1989). *Emerging literacy: Young children learn to read and write.* Newark, DE: International Reading Association.

Student saboteurs. (1989, May 10). *Education Week,* p. 3.

Teale, W. H., & Martinez, M. G. (1988). Getting on the right road to reading: Bringing books and young children together in the classroom. *Young Children, 44*(1), 10–15.

Throne, J. (1988). Becoming a kindergarten of readers? *Young Children, 43*(6), 10–16.

Tudge, J., & Caruso, D. (1988). Cooperative problem solving in the classroom: Enhancing young children's cognitive development. *Young Children, 44*(1), 46–52.

Warren, R. M. (1977). *Caring: Supporting children's growth.* Washington, DC: NAEYC.

Weaver, C. (1988). *Reading process and practice: From socio-psycholinguistics to whole language.* Portsmouth, NH: Heinemann.

White, S. (1975, March/April). Social implications of I.Q. *National Elementary School Principal, 10,* 10–14.

Willert, M. K., & Kamii, C. (1985). Reading in kindergarten: Direct vs. indirect teaching. *Young Children, 40*(4), 3–9.

Bibliography

American Educational Research Association, American Psychological Association, and National Council on Measurement in Education. (1985). *Standards for educational and psychological testing*. Washington, DC: Author.

American Federation of Teachers. (1988, July). Standardized testing in kindergarten. 1988 Convention Policy Resolution. In *AFT convention report* (pp. 58–59). Washington, DC: Author.

Association for Supervision and Curriculum Development. (1988). *A resource guide to public school early childhood programs*. Alexandria, VA: Author.

Berrueta-Clement, J. R., Schweinhart, L. J., Barnett, W. S., Epstein, A. S., & Weikart, D. P. (1984). *Changed lives: The effects of the Perry Preschool Program on youths through age 19*. Ypsilanti, MI: High/Scope.

Boehm, A. E. (1985). Review of Brigance K and 1 Screen. In J. V. Michael, Jr. (Ed.), *Ninth mental measurements yearbook* (Vol. 1, pp. 223–225). Lincoln, NE: Buros Institute of Mental Measurements.

Bradley, R. (1985). Review of Gesell School Readiness Test. In J. V. Michael, Jr. (Ed.), *Ninth mental measurements yearbook* (Vol. 1, pp. 609–610). Lincoln, NE: Buros Institute of Mental Measurements.

California State Department of Education. (1988). *Here they come: Ready or not. Report of the School Readiness Task Force*. Sacramento: Author.

Cannell, J. J. (1989). *How public educators cheat on standardized achievement tests*. Albuquerque, NM: Friends for Education.

Carini, P. F. (1975). *Observation and description: An alternative methodology for the investigation of human phenomena*. Grand Forks: University of North Dakota.

Charlesworth, R. (1989). "Behind" before they start? Deciding how to deal with the risk of kindergarten "failure." *Young Children, 44*(3), 5–13.

Courtney, R., Garry, M., Graves, C., Hughes, M., & McInnes, J. (1979). *Language development reading*. Scarborough, Ontario: Nelson/Canada Ltd.

CTB/McGraw-Hill. (1981). *Comprehensive Tests of Basic Skills*. New York: McGraw-Hill.

CTB/McGraw-Hill. (1985). *California Achievement Tests*. New York: McGraw-Hill.

Cunningham, A. E. (1988). *Eeny, meeny, miny, moe: Testing policy and practice in early childhood*. Berkeley, CA: National Commission on Testing and Public Policy.

Darling-Hammond, L., & Wise, A. E. (1985). Beyond standardization: State standards and school improvement. *The Elementary School Journal, 85*, 315–336.

Denton, J. J., & Tooke, D. J. (1981–82, Winter). Examining learner cognitive attainment as a basis for assessing student teachers. *Action in Teacher Education, 4*(4), 39–45.

Dewey, J. (1964). The child and the curriculum. In R. D. Archambault (Ed.), *John Dewey on education: Selected writing*. New York: The Modern Library. (Original work published 1902)

Dorr-Bremme, D. W., & Herman, J. L. (1986). *Assessing student achievement: A profile of classroom practices*. Los Angeles: Center for the Study of Evaluation.

Durkin, D. (1987). Testing in the kindergarten. *The Reading Teacher, 40*(8), 766–770.

Educational Research Service. (1986). Kindergarten programs and practices in public schools. *Principal, 65*(5), 22–23.

Elkind, D. (1987). *Miseducation: Preschoolers at risk*. New York: Knopf.

Farr, R., & Carey, R. (1986). *Reading: What can be measured?* Newark, DE: International Reading Association.

Gardner, E. F., Madden, R., Rudman, H. C., Karlsen, B., Merwin, J. C., Callis, R., & Collins, C. S. (1984). *Stanford Achievement Test Series handbook of instructional strategies*. Orlando, FL: Harcourt Brace Jovanovich (Psycological Corporation).

Gardner, E. F., Madden, R., Rudman, H. C., Karlsen, B., Merwin, J. C., Callis, R., & Collins, C. S. (1985). *Stanford Achievement Test Series technical data report*. Orlando, FL: Harcourt Brace Jovanovich (Psychological Corporation).

Gardner, E. F., Rudman, H. C., Karlsen, B., & Merwin, J. C. (1983). *Stanford Achievement Test index of instructional objectives* (Primary 1, 2, & 3). Orlando, FL: Harcourt Brace Jovanovich (Psychological Corporation).

Goodwin, W., & Driscoll, L. (1980). *Handbook for measurement and evaluation in early childhood education*. San Francisco: Jossey-Bass.

Goswami, D., & Stillman, P. R. (Eds.). (1987). *Reclaiming the classroom*. Portsmouth, NH: Heinemann.

Gould, S. (1981). *The mismeasure of man*. New York: Norton.

Gredler, G. R. (1984). Transition classes: A viable alternative for the at-risk child? *Psychology in the Schools, 21*, 463–470.

Haines, J., Ames, L. B., & Gillespie, C. (1980). *The Gesell preschool test manual*. Lumberville, PA: Modern Learning Press.

Hieronymus, A. N., Lindquist, E. F., & Hoover, H. D. (1988). *Iowa Tests of Basic Skills*. Chicago: Riverside Publishing.

Hilliard, A. (1975). The strengths and weaknesses of cognitive tests of young children. In J. D. Andrews (Ed.), *One child indivisible* (pp. 17–33). Washington, DC: NAEYC.

International Reading Association. (1986). Literacy development and pre-first grade: A joint statement of concerns about present practices in pre-first grade reading instruction and recommendations for improvement. *Childhood Education, 63*, 110–111.

Kagan, S. L. (1988). Public policy report. Current reforms in early childhood education: Are we addressing the issues? *Young Children, 43*(2), 27–32.

Katz, L., Raths, J., & Torres, R. (1987). *A place called kindergarten.* Urbana, IL: ERIC Clearinghouse on Elementary and Early Childhood Education. (ERIC Document Reproduction Service No. ED 280 595)

Kaufman, N. (1985). Review of Gesell School Readiness Test. In J. V. Michael, Jr. (Ed.), *Ninth mental measurements yearbook* (Vol. 1, pp. 607–608). Lincoln, NE: Buros Institute of Mental Measurements.

Madaus, G. (1985). Test scores as administrative mechanisms in educational policy. *Phi Delta Kappan, 66,* 611–618.

Medina, Z., & Neill, D. M. (1988). *Fallout from the testing explosion: How 100 million standardized exams undermine equity and excellence in America's public schools.* Cambridge, MA: National Center for Fair and Open Testing.

Mehan, H. (1979). *Learning lessons.* Cambridge, MA: Harvard University Press.

Meier, D. (1984). "Getting tough" in the schools. *Dissent, 31,* 61–70.

Meisels, S. J. (1987). Uses and abuses of developmental screening and school readiness testing. *Young Children, 42*(2), 4–6, 68–73.

Meisels, S. J. (1989). *Developmental screening in early childhood: A guide* (3rd ed.). Washington, DC: NAEYC.

Naglieri, J. J. (1985). Review of Gesell School Readiness Test. In J. V. Michael, Jr. (Ed.), *Ninth mental measurements yearbook* (Vol. 1, pp. 608–609). Lincoln, NE: Buros Institute of Mental Measurements.

National Association of Early Childhood Specialists in State Departments of Education. (1987). *Unacceptable trends in kindergarten entrance and placement.* Lincoln, NE: Author.

National Center for Fair and Open Testing. (1987, Fall). North Carolina legislature drops exams for 1st, 2nd graders. *FairTest Examiner,* p. 3.

Orlich, D. C. (1989). Education reforms: Mistakes, misconceptions, miscues. *Phi Delta Kappan, 70,* 512–517.

Plummer, D. L., Lineberger, M. H., & Graziano, W. G. (1986). The academic and social consequences of grade retention: A convergent analysis. In L. G. Katz (Ed.), *Current topics in early childhood education* (Vol. 6, pp. 224–252). Norwood, NJ: Ablex.

Prescott, G. A., Balow, I. H., Hogan, T. P., & Farr, R. C. (1986). *Metropolitan Achievement Test, MAT6.* Orlando: Harcourt Brace Jovanovich (Psychological Corporation).

Robinson, J. (1988). *The baby boards: A parents' guide to preschool and primary school entrance tests.* New York: Arco.

Rosenblatt, L. M. (1978). *The reader, the text, the poem: The transactional theory of the literary work.* Carbondale, IL: Southern Illinois University Press.

Salganik, L. H. (1985). Why testing reforms are so popular and how they are changing education. *Phi Delta Kappan, 66,* 607–610.

Shepard, L. A., & Smith, M. L. (1985, March). *Boulder Valley kindergarten study: Retention practices and retention effects.* Boulder, CO: Boulder Valley Public Schools.

Shepard, L., & Smith, M. (1986). Synthesis of research on school readiness and kindergarten retention. *Educational Leadership, 44*(3), 78–86.

Shepard, L. A., & Smith, M. L. (1987). Effects of kindergarten retention at the end of first grade. *Psychology in the Schools, 24,* 346–357.

Shepard, L. A., & Smith, M. L. (1988). Escalating academic demand in kindergarten: Counterproductive policies. *The Elementary School Journal, 89,* 135–145.

Smith, S. D., & Auger, K. (1985–86, Winter). Conflict or cooperation? Keys to success in partnerships in teacher education. *Action in Teacher Education, 7*(4), 1–9.

Teale, W., Hiebert, E., & Chittenden, E. (1987). Assessing young children's literacy development. *The Reading Teacher, 40,* 772–776.

Timar, T. B., & Kirp, D. L. (1989). Education reform in the 1980s: Lessons from the states. *Phi Delta Kappan, 70,* 504–511.

Tyson-Bernstein, H. (1988). *A conspiracy of good intentions: America's textbook fiasco.* Washington, DC: Council for Basic Education.

U. S. Department of Education. (1988). *Creating responsible and responsive accountability systems* (Report of the OERI State Accountability Study Group). Washington, DC: Author.

Valencia, S., & Pearson, P. (1987). Reading assessment: Time for a change. *The Reading Teacher, 40,* 726–732.

Warger, C. (Ed.). (1988). *A resource guide to public schools' early childhood programs.* Alexandria, VA: Association for Supervision and Curriculum Development.

Waters, E. (1985). Review of Gesell School Readiness Test. In J. V. Michael, Jr. (Ed.), *Ninth mental measurements yearbook* (Vol. 1, pp. 610–611). Lincoln, NE: Buros Institute of Mental Measurements.

Willie, C. V. (1985). The problem of standardized testing in a free and pluralistic society. *Phi Delta Kappan, 66,* 626–628.

Wise, A. E. (1988). Legislated learning revisited. *Phi Delta Kappan, 69,* 328–333.

Yatvin, J. (1987). Playing the testing game. *Educational Leadership, 45*(3), 88–89.

Information About NAEYC

NAEYC is . . .

. . . a membership-supported organization of people committed to fostering the growth and development of children from birth through age 8. Membership is open to all who share a desire to serve and act on behalf of the needs and rights of young children.

NAEYC provides . . .

. . . educational services and resources to adults who work with and for children, including

- *Young Children, the* journal for early childhood educators
- **Books, posters, brochures, and videos** to expand your knowledge and commitment to young children, with topics including infants, curriculum, research, discipline, teacher education, and parent involvement
- An **Annual Conference** that brings people from all over the country to share their expertise and advocate on behalf of children and families
- **Week of the Young Child** celebrations sponsored by NAEYC Affiliate Groups across the nation to call public attention to the needs and rights of children and families
- **Insurance plans** for individuals and programs
- **Public affairs information** for knowledgeable advocacy efforts at all levels of government and through the media
- **The National Academy of Early Childhood Programs**, a voluntary accreditation system for high-quality programs for children
- The **Information Service,** a computer-based, centralized source of information sharing, distribution, and collaboration

For free information about membership, publications, or other NAEYC services . . .
. . . call NAEYC at 202-232-8777 or 800-424-2460 or write to NAEYC, 1834 Connecticut Ave., N.W., Washington, DC 20009-5786.